THE WORLD'S MONEY
How it works

WILLIAM M. CLARKE
AND GEORGE PULAY

LONDON · GEORGE ALLEN AND UNWIN LTD

PRINTED IN GREAT BRITAIN
in 11 *point Times Roman*
BY UNWIN BROTHERS LIMITED
WOKING AND LONDON

Preface

This book has been written primarily for people who are interested in knowing about the world's monetary crises, yet who do not have enough basic knowledge to follow all the financial comments in the press, on radio and on television. It is a simple guide to the way the international monetary system works today and how it might work in the future. Since the book has been completed, gyrations on Wall Street have once again raised the spectre of another 1929. Whilst we cannot foresee what is likely to happen we have tried to highlight the differences between then and now in Chapter 14. Although it can be dipped into, the book has been deliberately designed to be read as a whole, starting with a simple monetary framework and gradually progressing to rather harder material. Financial phrases have been explained when first introduced and the index at the back of the book should help readers to find relevant explanations. As a final test, we have included in the last chapter several press extracts giving the reader a chance to 'test' his newly acquired knowledge.

Our thanks go to a variety of people and institutions; to Miss Frances Cairncross, economic correspondent of the *Observer*, to Mr Tom Nisbet (formerly assistant editor *Times Business News*) and especially to Mr Hamish McRae, Assistant Editor of the *Banker* who played a major role in getting the whole project off the ground and onto paper.

The non-expert has been equally valuable. Mr Lee Montague who, in spite of giving one of the shrewdest financial monologues in recent theatre history (in 'The Latent Heterosexual' by Paddy Chayevsky at the Aldwych), still claims nearly total ignorance, has been kind enough to act as a voluntary guinea-pig and to help us simplify the indigestible. For the lumpy bits that remain, only we are to blame.

We must also thank the editor of the *Director* for permission to reproduce material in Chapter 9 which previously appeared in that journal; the editor of the *Evening Standard* for permission to quote an article by Lord Kilbracken in Chapter 4; all the newspapers who have been kind enough to let us reproduce special articles in the last chapter; and not least some of the international organizations whose own material has been of considerable assistance.

W.M.C.
G.P.

June, 1970

Contents

A
HOW THE WORLD'S MONEY WORKS

Chapter 1

THE USES OF WORLD MONEY

International finance is a mystery to most men and women.
But even schoolboys and politicians know that this has been
a year of crisis in world financial markets—and that the
well-being of millions of ordinary people was jeopardized.
And yet—thanks to the foundations that were laid at
Bretton Woods years ago—those crises did not lead to
panic and depression. Somehow, we overcame each one. We
learned from each one. So we are stronger today for the
trouble that we met and the trouble that we mastered
together.

Thus former President Johnson speaking in Washington three
months before he handed over to President Nixon and at the
end of twelve months of financial tensions—the devaluation of
the pound, the international run on gold, the dramatic drop in
France's gold reserves. His audience: finance ministers and
central bankers from over a hundred nations. His message:
that the world had come close to the abyss but had been saved
by international co-operation. Yet how many really knew how
or why? Or even cared?

The fact is that recent world currency crises have had a
peculiar air of unreality about them. In the 1930s, queues
of unemployed and needless poverty were enough to convince
the most fervent optimist of the shakiness of the whole money
system. Nowadays we watch the financial drama unfold,
comfortably, in front of a television set. We see central bankers
scurrying from one international centre to another. The prosperity of mankind is at stake, we are told, as we hurriedly
switch to another channel. And until it hits us where it hurts—in
our pockets—few of us are likely to get worked up about it.

This book has been written for the few 'schoolboys and
politicians' who do not know, as well as for the thousands of

13

others who remain unaware. For while prosperity may have been saved by international co-operation, the jargon, the technical language, has become daily more complex. And complexity dulls curiosity. Yet the same questions still crop up. Why do nations hoard gold? What is the point of digging gold out of the ground in one part of the globe and burying it in another? Why has France so often been the odd man out? What exactly is the Bretton Woods system? What is this so-called new world money? How serious is the present situation and how close has our economic system been to disaster? Could the experience of the 1930s still be repeated? In a word, what's behind all these regular meetings of grim-faced central bankers in the various financial centres, Basle one month, Frankfurt the next, Washington the month after that?

We shall try to answer most of them. But we must start with a simpler one. What use is international money and how different is it from the cash in our pockets. Take ordinary money first: the notes and coins we know. We can quickly discover three main uses. One is that, without it, none of us could get beyond bartering one thing for another—all the complex exchanges of our society would be impossible. Another is that money helps us to put a value on things and compare the value of one thing with that of another. This in turn helps us to decide what is worth producing and what is not: that is, what we *want* to exchange and what we do not. These two are the most important functions of money: we use them every time we step outside the front door. There is also a third: it enables us to store wealth—if we do not want to use it immediately we can keep it until we do.

So in these various ways money acts as a lubricant for the whole system. Economists have their own words for these different functions. They call them 'medium of exchange', 'unit of account' and 'store of wealth'. In the first two uses there is no real substitute for money; nothing can take its place and do the job so well. But for the third, certainly for longish perods, money is not very good itself. We know only too well that its buying power seems inevitably to decline over the years. In the United States its value has recently been going down by around

14

5 per cent a year; in Britain by 3 or 4 per cent. So if we want to store value for a long period, almost certainly we would do better to buy paintings, houses, shares or common stock—anything for which there is a lasting demand. For short periods, however, money is a perfectly satisfactory way of storing wealth. If we are likely to spend money within a few days of getting it the loss is negligible.

What then about international money? What does that do? The answer is: exactly the same as the ordinary stuff: it performs the three functions we have already explained. The only difference is that it is used for settling debts between governments or people in *different* countries instead of between people in the *same* country. Countries need to exchange goods with each other almost as much as individuals. Britain needs to buy half its food from abroad, not to mention the raw materials from which its exports are made. Even the United States, with far less dependence on foreign trade, buys $36,000 million's worth a year from other countries. Just like individual producers, countries have to have some method of putting a value to their products so as to know what they ought to make themselves and what they ought to buy from others. And (this is the third use of money) they need to have some way of tiding themselves over if from time to time their exports don't cover their imports: so they keep gold and foreign exchange reserves. The parallel even holds true in that some kinds of international money are not a very good way of holding wealth for a long period: overseas investments would bring in a greater return. If a country does not want to run down its reserves to pay for too many imports she can always sell off foreign investments. This is roughly what Britain has been doing since 1964, when the Government started selling the American shares she had held since the last war.

To carry out these functions efficiently money, whether national or international, must have several qualities:

It must be acceptable by everybody: nobody (except possibly a miser) wants to have money if he can't pass it on to someone else.

15

It must be convenient to carry and store: which means it must be valuable in relation to size and weight.

It must be of consistent quality and ideally it should also be indestructible: traveller's cheques are an obvious way in which paper money has been given this advantage.

If possible, too, money should have some intrinsic value: in some way or other it must be useful in itself.

Before looking closely at developments in international money, we must have a preliminary look at how the use of ordinary money has developed. Throughout the ages all kinds of things have been used as money, all having, to a greater or lesser extent, most of these characteristics. Early in man's history all exchange was by barter and the first kinds of money were just popular barter items. Cattle were widely used, despite their obvious disadvantages. Sometimes ornaments were employed, like the cowrie shells, currency of the South Sea Islands. Even today, if for some reason or other people become suspicious of conventional money, some form of barter item will take its place. Cigarettes, for example, were widely acceptable in Germany after the Second World War. And ball-point pens can start a useful exchange behind the Iron Curtain even today.

But by far the most convenient form of money was found to be the precious metals, in particular gold and silver. They were useful in themselves, easily carried, difficult to destroy but at the same time easy to split into the size required. Above all (and in fact because of these features) they were acceptable both at home and abroad.

The precious metals by themselves had, however, two grave disadvantages. They were liable to debasement and they had to be weighed each time they were exchanged. It was to get round these problems that metal was minted into coins. This gave a guarantee (admittedly inadequate) both of weight and quality and coins became by far the most convenient form of money. But it also introduced a disadvantage. It meant that metal was no longer completely international: the coins of one country were not necessarily acceptable in another. But they did at least have one thing in common—their value roughly approximated

16

to the value of the metal in them. This gave a basis on which coins could be exchanged, an advantage that began to disappear as soon as bank notes were introduced to replace coins.

When bank notes were introduced, the obligation to pay coin replaced the actual coin itself. But this had far-reaching results. For in the fifteenth and sixteenth centuries the newly emerging banks (or goldsmiths, as many of them were) discovered that they could issue notes—promises to pay coin—beyond the amount of coin that they had in their vaults. They could safely do this because they knew that everybody who held their notes would not bring them along for payment at the same time. (Sometimes they misjudged it, with disastrous results for their depositors, and sometimes, themselves.) Of course, unless they were dishonest, they had to have assets of some sort to back their notes. As time went on, and largely to overcome both dishonesty and private misjudgements, the tendency was for all notes to be issued by the government or central bank and to be guaranteed by the State. The value of these notes—like the value of the coins they replaced—remained tied to metal for several centuries. Indeed until 1914 almost all currencies were either tied to gold (which had replaced silver as the most favoured metal) or tied to currencies that themselves had a fixed price in gold.

This is no longer so. Today the ordinary person cannot wander into a bank and demand gold for bank notes at the official price. Notes are pure tokens. It is difficult to say just why they are valuable. Part of the answer lies in the fact that they are scarce, but some economists explain their value by pointing out that they are backed by the taxing power of the State. If the government really had to redeem the notes in, say cigarettes, it could do so. The basic fact, however, is that (provided too many are not issued) the public believes (and is backed in its belief by the law) that they will be readily accepted by everyone else; that is, they are 'legal tender'.

The final stage in the development of money was when bank deposits came to be thought of as money. Today the major part of the money in any western country is in fact bank deposits.

There is after all no fundamental difference between paying a bill by cheque and paying in cash. Money in your bank account is just as good as notes in your pocket. Even a loan, or an overdraft counts. Just as a central bank can increase the amount of money by printing more notes, a commercial bank can do so by allowing its customers to overdraw. This in turn means that if the government wants to control the amount of money in the country, it has to control bank lending.

Virtually all these stages in the development of ordinary money have their parallel in international money. The only difference is that the final stage has not been developed to the same extent: there is still no world central bank controlling the total amount of international currency in circulation. In other respects the stages are the same. Originally, countries[1] used to barter and many of them still do from time to time. Barter deals, for example, are often used when trading with the Soviet Union, and Rhodesia recently found that barter provided a way of offsetting economic sanctions. Later, as barter became too restrictive, countries began to use the more sophisticated method of exchanging each other's coins. If one country found it had too much of another's coinage it could always melt it down and mint the metal into its own currency. But with the growth of paper money, the position became more complicated: one country could hardly melt down another's bank notes and the notes themselves would be useless in a country where the bank was unknown and where they could not be presented for payment. As a result most countries came to use notes for domestic money and metal (gold or silver) for international transactions. There was, of course, no sudden change-over, though with the large expansion of trade in the nineteenth century it was plainly a convenient way of using gold (silver was already being superseded economically).

We shall explain in a later chapter how different ways of arranging and controlling international payments developed:

[1] Some readers may be puzzled by the reference here and in the following pages to transactions between 'countries'; we are in essence using 'country' as an abbreviation for the monetary authority (government plus central bank) of a nation. Exactly how this relates to transactions between *individuals* (or firms) of differing nationalities will be explained in Chapter 2.

the start of the gold standard, the attempts to re-introduce it after the First World War, the crisis of 1929–31, the establishment of the Bretton Woods system after the Second World War and the more recent crises and solutions. What we want to do first is to outline in simple terms what is used to make international payments today. Gold is still at the centre of the system. All currencies are fixed to it in some way or other. In addition the pound and the dollar—the so called 'reserve currencies'—have been regarded 'as good as gold' in so far as they have been substituted for it in international payments. Finally the International Monetary Fund which was set up after World War Two to run the system, makes loans, known as 'drawing-rights', to countries that are in difficulties.

Thus there are three basic ways that bills (that is, outstanding balances) between countries can be settled. They can be paid in gold. They can be settled in national currencies. Or they can be paid by some form of credit arrangement. The first is the simplest. Some countries prefer to be paid (and hold their reserves) in that way. France, for example, even insists on having gold due to it shipped into the country. Others are prepared to leave the gold in the debtor country provided it is assigned to them. Thus a significant share of the gold in the vaults of the Federal Reserve Bank of New York is really owned by other countries. Russia and the Soviet bloc, who are not members of the International Monetary Fund, find that gold provides them with a way of buying from the West, a point illustrated by Russia's heavy sales of gold in the early 1960s in order to pay for Canadian wheat.

If payment is to be made in currencies which should be used? A country can pay in its own, if its creditor is prepared to accept it. The chances are that although this may be possible to a certain extent, the country owed the money may not want to have too much of that particular currency on its hands. At present, therefore, most countries keep only small working balances of other countries' money. If they get too much they convert it into gold, dollars or pounds. The latter two reserve currencies are in a special position and between them account for just under 30 per cent of the total of international money.

19

Finally, a brief word about credit arrangements. These fall into two broad groups—those organized through the IMF, and those arranged formally between individual countries. In the case of the IMF loans there is a set of rules governing the amount of money a country can borrow. This is related to the size of the subscription it pays, which in turn is linked to such factors as the amount of its imports, the size of its economy, and so on. (A country can usually borrow up to twice the value of its subscription.) The more a country borrows the more closely its economic policies are scrutinized by the IMF. But for most countries this is the only way they can expect to borrow international money.

In the case of the other kind of credit, the informal borrowing arrangements, there is no fixed limit to the amount a country can borrow, nor indeed any procedure for forcing a country to follow certain economic policies. But there can be problems in finding countries prepared to lend money. Remember the old joke that bankers only lend money to people who do not need it? In fact this has in recent years been slightly modified by British experience. Because of the importance of the pound to the whole system (so many people still use it and hold it) countries have been prepared to chip in and lend money. On one dramatic day in November 1964, Lord Cromer, then Governor of the Bank of England was able, with the help of the US Federal Reserve, to raise $3,000 million from the world's central banks. The drama, however, must not be allowed to obscure the fact that the other countries were not really taking any great risk as the money they lent was still guaranteed against gold and they probably had little choice.

Chapter 2

HOW ARE PAYMENTS MADE?

*A foreign exchange dealers' office during a busy spell is the
nearest thing to Bedlam I have struck.*
—Harold Wincott, 1958.

In the last chapter we were talking about international money
as the money used to settle outstanding debts between countries.
But these kinds of payments are made by governments, not
people. The individual transactions are usually carried out
by thousands of different traders rather than by countries as a
whole. There are some exceptions, of course, particularly in
Communist countries, where governments and their agencies
undertake trade overseas. As we have already seen, it was the
Russian Government (not individual importers) that bought
Canadian wheat, paying for it in gold. But when trade is between
people or firms, as in the free world, payment has to be made in
local currency. Even if you can persuade a Paris taxi driver to
accept pounds or dollars he will still have to take them to his
bank and swap them for francs before the money is any use to
him. The same holds true if a company wants to buy foreign
goods. As a result the banks have built up an international
network for exchanging different national currencies. Thus the
bills that countries as a whole (or rather their governments)
have to foot are basically the *balance* (plus or minus) of all the
various deals that their residents are carrying out. In this chapter we shall try to show how the banks handle these thousands
of international payments, each one demanding an exchange
of currencies—in short, how the foreign exchange market works.
    Let us take a simple example. If we have decided to take a
holiday in France, we need some francs before we go. We ask
for them at the bank, the bank works out the rate of exchange,
debits our account by the equivalent amount of pounds or
dollars, and hands us the franc notes. But this simple description

of an apparently simple process begs two important questions: how does the bank know by how much to debit our account (i.e. how much francs are worth in terms of other currencies); and where does it get the notes from anyway? The first question we shall be dealing with in a later chapter on how exchange rates are determined. Here we are simply concerned with the mechanics of the foreign exchange market—how banks get other countries' money.

It is just possible that the bank already has some francs—another customer may have come back from France and cashed his spare notes. It is possible too for the head office of the bank to write to its French branch or agents and get them to post some. But in the case of a local British bank the chances are that it will get them from the foreign bank note market in London. Though one or two banks act as wholesalers in this market, most probably it will go to an old-established merchant bank in the City of London, Brown, Shipley & Co.

It was during the 1950s that Brown, Shipley & Co. gradually built up its dominant position in the market for foreign bank notes. This is a wholesale market where the few franc notes we happen to want will be lumped together with all the other notes our own bank needs. Thus normally Brown, Shipley & Co. would not deal in the sort of figures that a private individual would want: certainly not in the major currencies. Altogether it swaps about £35 millions' worth of notes a year in something like 140 currencies. It has a network of correspondent (agent) banks all over the world and it trades with them in any notes that it cannot manage to balance out in London. The notes themselves are moved around by air freight or even by post.

Of course notes make up only a small share of the total money used in domestic trade,[1] and a still smaller share in international trade. Even people going on holiday abroad usually take the bulk of their money in travellers' cheques rather than notes. So nearly all currency exchange is in the form of paper transfers. This means that it appears more nebulous: there is not any one market centre, parcels are not sent back and forth—often there

[1] For example of the total money supply in the United Kingdom at the end of 1969 £3,000m. was made up of notes and coin, £13,000m. of bank deposits.

is only a cable message—and instead of there being one main firm, there are hundreds. But the principle is exactly the same.

Take an actual deal. The distributor of a range of French motor cars in London has to pay for his next shipment. Pounds are useless to the French manufacturer, he can't pay his wage bill with them, and the distributor has to pay in francs. He therefore instructs his bank to make the payment in francs and to deduct the sterling equivalent from his account. In fact the deal could work the other way round: the importer could give the French manufacturer a sterling cheque, which in turn would be cashed in the French bank and converted into francs. Either way the result is the same. In the first case the British bank has to buy francs for pounds; in the second the French one has to sell pounds and buy francs. It is at this point—where one currency has to be exchanged for another—that the foreign exchange market comes into the picture.

The feudal system was once described as 'chaos, quite well organized'. The same could well be said for the foreign exchange market. First of all, there is no one centre where the banks all meet to do their business.[1] In this respect the foreign exchange market is unlike the stock market. Instead banks throughout the world have a so-called dealers' room. These rooms, concentrated in the main financial centres of the world—London, New York, Frankfurt, Paris, Zurich and others—are linked with each other by telephone and telex. All deals are done through this complex network.

To give some idea of the complexity of the network, there are some 170 banks and other firms licensed to deal in foreign exchange in London alone. In London there are also nine broking firms through which most of the business is done. These brokerage houses make a living by matching up buyer and seller. In New York there are fewer brokerage firms—the banks tend to deal direct with each other to a much greater extent—but there, as in the other financial centres, the set-up is basically the same.

[1] There used to be one in London. Before the First World War the heads of the leading merchant banks used to meet at the Royal Exchange (opposite the Bank of England) to fix rates of exchange.

23

The size of these dealers' rooms varies and not all the banks licensed to deal in foreign exchange do so every day. A small bank might have one part-time dealer, a big one half a dozen or more. The dealer himself is a key man. In theory his job is simple. In practice it results in what the late British financial journalist, Mr Harold Wincott, once described as 'the nearest thing to Bedlam I have struck'. But perhaps the best description of what it really means to be a foreign exchange dealer comes from a dealer himself, Jack R. Higgins, in a symposium *A day in the Life of a Banker:*

'Calls from customers, calls from foreign banks overseas, calls from the brokers. Some merely seeking information, some seeking rates on which to base their day's work. There will be calls from Paris, Amsterdam, Copenhagen, Brussels, Hamburg and many other financial centres. Some with genuine propositions, some hoping for an advantageous quotation somewhere in the list . . . The babel rises a few decibels as the linguists join the chorus. Rates are being quoted in French, Italian and probably German. Each operator will be dealing with the requirements of his own particular caller whilst keeping his ear cocked to any possible changes in rates by his colleagues as they effect their deals. . . .' [1]

From this extract many complications become apparent. The dealer has an endless string of questions facing him. He is buying odd amounts of currency, sometimes odd currencies, with the rates moving every minute. The number of permutations of prices between even a small number of currencies is obvious. Some people even make a living out of the tiny difference in rates in the different financial centres—this is called arbitrage. But perhaps the biggest complication comes from the fact that currencies are often bought in advance, that is, for delivery in several months' time. The reason for this is probably best explained by going back to our car importer.

Suppose he signs a contract to take 10,000 French cars for delivery over the next three months and for payment (at fixed

[1] Institute of Bankers, 1963.

prices in French francs) at the end of that period. What happens if during those three months Britain decides to devalue the pound in terms of francs? He will have to pay more (in terms of pounds) for the cars, which he may well have already sold at a sterling price based on the earlier rate of exchange. So what he does in effect is to insure against the currency risk by getting hold of, or at least arranging to get hold of, his francs in advance —in this case for delivery in three months' time—on the forward market. He then knows that whatever happens to sterling he will be covered. The technical name for the ordinary currency rate is the 'spot' rate, while there are a number of 'forward' rates for the major currencies, of which the most usually quoted are one month, three months and a year.

This is all very well, you may say, but are there not other complications in international trade finance—for example, what are 'bills of exchange' and how do they fit into this picture? The answer is that they are just a system for financing trade both within countries and between them. Just like cheques the funds still have to be cleared through the foreign exchange market. But as they are still a most important part of the trade mechanism, it may help to take a brief look at them.

If a company wants a short-term loan to cover the cost of some goods it has bought while they are in transit or perhaps until they are resold, it can give the supplier a cheque and get an overdraft from its own bank. Equally it could give the supplier a post-dated cheque, dated say, three months ahead. Crudely this is what a bill of exchange is. The trouble with post-dated cheques is that the supplier has to stand the credit till they mature. Bills of exchange can however be 'discounted', that is, presented to a bank in exchange for cash, but slightly less cash than the amount of money on the face of the bill. This difference is in effect the interest that the bank charges for advancing the money straightaway.

International bills of exchange are just a development of national ones, and work in much the same way. They were developed in the last century by the British merchant banks and became the main means of finance for international trade. There are various refinements but basically the bills are guaranteed by

25

leading merchant banks (the process is known as 'accepting', hence the name 'accepting houses' for seventeen of the leading merchant banks)[1] and can then be cashed (or 'discounted') at certain discount houses[2] which specialize in such bills of exchange. The bills can also be used by banks as a type of security recognized by the Bank of England against which they are allowed to lend more money.

This is all rather technical. The important thing to realize is that funds transferred between countries by both cheques and bills have to be cleared through the foreign exchange market.

But the foreign exchange market is not only called on to swap money because of international trade in goods. There are two other main reasons why people in different countries want to exchange money: 'invisibles' and 'capital transfers'. The rest of this chapter looks at these two in turn.

The somewhat sinister title of *invisibles* is really a convenient umbrella word for a whole hotch-potch of deals which cannot easily be classified elsewhere. A large portion of these invisible payments are payments for 'services'. If you go and have your hair cut you have 'bought' a service. If you buy a steak in a restaurant for £1, you may be paying 7s for the steak itself, and the rest for the service of cooking it. Similarly there is international trade in services, the most important of which are such things as air and sea travel, insurance, and banking itself. But there are other less obvious ones: overseas singing tours by pop stars, foreign royalties of writers, fees paid by foreign clients to advertising agencies, even the foreign income of casinos. In other words 'invisible' earnings arise basically from the provision of services of all kinds to foreigners, and from the income

[1] The names of these seventeen merchant banks are: Baring Brothers & Co., Wm. Brandt's Sons & Co., Brown, Shipley & Co., Charterhouse Japhet & Thomasson; Antony Gibbs & Sons; Guinness Mahon & Co., Hill Samuel & Co.; Kleinwort, Benson; Lazard Brothers & Co., Morgan Grenfell & Co., Samuel Montague & Co., Rea Brothers; N. M. Rothschild & Sons; J. Henry Schroder Wagg & Co.; S. G. Warburg & Co.

[2] The leading discount houses in the City of London are: Alexanders Discount Co.; Allen, Harvey & Ross; Cater, Ryder & Co.; Clive Discount & Co.; Gerrard & National Discount Co.; Gillett Bros Discount Co.; Jessel, Toynbee & Co.; King & Shaxson; Seccombe, Marshall & Campion; Smith, St. Aubyn & Co.; Union Discount Co.

from investments abroad (whether in shares or factories). Another major type of invisible trade is tourism; some countries manage to pay for almost all their imports just out of the overseas earnings of tourism—the Bahamas are a good example. And both Italy and Spain now rely considerably on their growing earnings from foreign tourists.

The other main type of invisible payments are interest and dividends from foreign investments. Here the 'service', if it can be called that, is the loan of the money for the investment. It is largely because of their massive investments overseas that the United States and Britain stand head and shoulders above all other countries in the world invisible league table. Curiously a foreign factory can be both an invisible and a visible earner. For example a US car subsidiary in England is an invisible export of America (because it sends back its profits) and a visible exporter for Britain (because it exports British-made cars).

But how does the United States get its British subsidiary in the first place? This brings us to the final reason why funds have to be exchanged: *capital transfers*. As with invisibles they take a multitude of forms. But they have one thing in common (and this is why they differ from both visible and invisible trade): no goods change hands, no service in the true sense of the word is performed. Instead an asset is created.

Governments, private firms and individuals all make capital transfers. Overseas investment by firms is the most obvious form of such a transfer—at any rate in Europe. One has only to look around to see some product built by a subsidiary company most probably of the US. Cars are a good example, with Ford (UK and German), Opel, Vauxhall, Simca and Rootes all owned by the big three American manufacturers. The oil companies all make massive investments throughout the world, with the European ones up in the same rank as the Americans. A sort of international language composed of words like Hoover, Persil and Nescafé, stands testimony to the importance of such overseas investment.

Foreign investment by private individuals is less remarkable. These investments fall into two groups. Most usually they are either shares in foreign companies—'portfolio' investment—or

27

foreign property. It is more difficult nowadays to make foreign investments than it used to be. Britain has introduced legislation where part of the proceeds of sales of foreign shares have to be sent back to the mother country. But there are still substantial transfers, which have to be cleared through the foreign exchange market. How else could someone going to live abroad take enough money to buy a new house and so on?

And so to government transfers. These are something of a special case. In recent years governments of the rich countries have increasingly made loans to the poorer nations. Sometimes, too, grants are made; these are the main type of capital transfer that do not result in an overseas asset being created for the country giving the money.

Capital transfers of all kinds are usually divided into two types, short-term and long-term. There is no hard and fast distinction, but if the money is generally intended to stay in the country for some time (as, for example, when a factory is being built) then it is considered long-term. If, on the other hand, it is merely resting there for a few days, perhaps to take advantage of higher interest rates, then it is short-term. Sometimes it is difficult to see which it is. A Middle East oil sheik investing on the Wall Street stock market might intend to keep his money there for years. But it would be risky to count on it, so this should probably be classified as a short-term investment.

So much for the detail. It is time to pick up our main thread again. To recap for a moment, we have discussed three main reasons why countries, or the individuals in those countries, have to pay each other money: to pay for goods imported; to pay for services supplied by other countries; and to make investments, both private and governmental, in other countries. Very often these payments involve an exchange of different currencies and a mechanism has been built up by the banks all over the world for swapping these currencies—the foreign exchange market. And we have seen, in the first chapter, that at the end of all these transactions the balance, plus or minus, has to be evened out by the governments. The task of the next chapter is to look at the basic reasons why these overall deficits and surpluses arise.

Chapter 3

WHY PAYMENTS ARE MADE

There is no commercial country in Europe of which the
approaching ruin has not frequently been foretold by the
pretended doctors of this system from an unfavourable
balance of trade. After all the anxiety, however, which
they have excited about this, after all the vain attempts of
almost all trading nations to turn that balance in their own
favour and against their neighbours, it does not appear that
any one nation in Europe has been in any respect im-
poverished by this cause. Every town and country, on the
contrary, in proportion as they have opened their ports to
all nations, instead of being ruined by this free trade . . .
have been enriched by it.
—Adam Smith, *The Wealth of Nations*, 1776.

Few newspaper readers in the late 1960s needed to be reminded
that something was wrong with Britain's balance of payments.
This apparently insoluble (though temporary) problem was
used as a scapegoat for just about every unpopular move the
Government made. It was blamed for higher taxes; it was
blamed for the fact that we had not been building enough
hospitals or schools, or not clearing the slums quickly enough;
it was cited every time the banks stopped lending money or
when house mortgage costs went up; and of course it was the
obvious reason for the £50 travel allowance between 1966 and
early 1970 and for the 1967 devaluation itself.

But if Britain's balance of payments for a time tended to
become something of a bore throughout the world, the United
States did not escape unscathed either. American companies
have had to cut down their flow of overseas investment (or
borrow abroad to pay for it); American aid to the underdeveloped world has been squeezed; and American tourists
have been persuaded to spend less abroad.

What brought such apparently rich countries to this state? Neither was exactly on the bread line. Britain is rich compared with many countries, while the United States's ability to find the resources to fight a major war, put men on the moon and increase the standard of living at home at one and the same time (whether all are desirable or not) has attracted the admiration (if also the envy) of the world. A visitor from Mars, would doubtless be amazed to hear that both countries had been in deficit—that neither had been paying their way. But it is quite true for the US and was true for Britain. The latter achieved a current payments surplus (or 'profit' if all the country's payments are added together) in only one year between 1964 and 1968, before moving into surplus again in 1969. The deficit was over £400 million in 1964, 1967 and 1968. The United States has, in a sense, done even worse with an annual 'loss' running at around $3,000 and $4,000 million since the 1950s. Admittedly it managed to move back into a small surplus in 1968 so honouring President Johnson's undertaking in his State of the Union message in January 1968, but this was only because of special circumstances. In the last chapter we talked of the three main reasons why countries pay each other money: payments for trade, payments for services, and capital investments. And we pointed out that the bill a deficit country had to foot was the result of all the different deals done by individuals in the country with people in other countries. The recent experience of both Britain and the US has been a good example of the different ways in which countries can end up with such a deficit.

But before we examine some of the recent accounts of these two countries it may help to look at the theoretical ways a deficit or surplus can arise. Take a country that is in balance. Either the amount of money the country has to pay out for goods and services bought from the rest of the world is paid for almost exactly by the amount of money received for the goods and services it supplies to others; or if there is a gap, it is covered by the investments the country makes or receives. Now let us see how this country can fall into deficit. In the first place, it may start to run a visible trade deficit—

buying more goods from overseas than it is exporting. This can happen for several reasons. It could be that its people suddenly decide that they want to spend their money on foreign goods. If this seems an odd idea, remember that the reverse is more common: the 'I'm backing Britain' campaign was in part an attempt to make people buy British products rather than foreign (even if the stickers did start to sprout from the back windows of Volkswagens). And a 'Buy Irish' campaign substantially reduced imports in Ireland in the early 1960s. Economists call these movements, whether government-inspired or spontaneous, 'changes in tastes'.

But a more likely reason for the worsening of the trade position is when, because of manufacturing and technical changes in the production, and demand for goods, goods of other countries become cheaper in world markets; or, as economists say, because of 'structural changes'. This can happen in many ways. A country with lower wages might start to make goods already made by other countries and find it can do so more cheaply. The decline of the Lancashire cotton industry—it once clothed half the world—was largely the result of low-cost producers like India, Japan and Hong Kong starting to make the same type of goods. Much the same thing happens when a technical advance takes place in a country enabling it to produce either better or cheaper goods for export. A more simple 'structural change' is when it just happens that the type of goods that the country has specialized in are no longer wanted, and it is not able (or cannot be bothered) to switch production to more modern demands. The growth of the Japanese shipbuilding industry since the last war at the expense of Britain and the US, shows how these various forces can combine to have a devasting effect on trading relationships. Japan not only had cheaper labour; it also concentrated on the growing market for giant tankers and bulk carriers, developing new techniques so that it could build these large ships cheaply. As a result, by 1968 it was building over half the world's shipping tonnage. In the same year British output was about a tenth of Japanese output and had fallen back to the 1945 level.

31

There is another more general reason why a country's trade position can worsen: if its overall level of prices rises faster than that of its trading partners. We need not concern ourselves with the initial reason for the rise in the price-level; it does not matter much whether it is sparked off by a wage increase, by manufacturers deciding that they want higher profit margins, or even by the inflationary policy of a government. If the general price-level rises, almost certainly export prices will go up too. Similarly, imports will become relatively cheaper. Now, it is just possible that this can benefit the trade account. If other countries do not mind paying more for the country's exports: and if people at home decide that despite the fact that foreign goods are relatively cheaper, they still want to buy things made by their own country, then the trade account will benefit. But the chances are that the shift in prices will also cause a shift in demand. This will mean that the country can't export as much and will import more. As a result the trade balance will slip into deficit. Economists explain such a trend by referring to 'price elasticities of demand'. What they mean is how much the demand for a product changes when its price goes up or down. The factors that affect such a change are complicated and depend on such things as the importance that people attach to the goods and the proportion of their income that they spend on them.

So far we have been talking about a country slipping into deficit because of a deterioration in its visible trade position. This is a frequent cause, but it is by no means the only one. As we saw earlier, countries also have to exchange money for other reasons than trade: for example, because of invisible services and government expenditure.

Let us take invisible services first. The main types of invisibles were set out in the last chapter and we explained that the term was really an umbrella word for a whole group of unrelated sorts of deals. In effect they are payments for services provided to or by foreigners. On any of these deals—be it royalties from books, the spending of tourists, banking earnings or interest from investments overseas—a country can be in surplus or deficit. And it can slip into deficit for the same reasons that its trade position can worsen; changes in tastes, structural changes, and differing rates of inflation. Sometimes this last factor is the most important. One has only to notice the way that British tourists hurry through France where food and hotels are expensive to get into Spain where they are cheaper to see how a high cost of living can affect tourist earnings. But banking (or for that matter pop star earnings) is not affected to the same extent by such considerations. With banking, structural changes are most important—that is, changes in the location of foreign banks and the business they do. The Americanization of European industry, for example, has been a major factor in persuading American banks to set up branches in London and elsewhere. And, clearly, the rise (and fall?) of the Beatles has been solely dependent on tastes.

Now we turn to a third element in a country's overseas payments. In official statistics government transactions are usually added into the invisible account, though logically we feel they should be separated from it. For Britain and the United States this part of the account is in deficit, though in the case of other countries, primarily Germany and Japan, the presence of foreign troops on their territory increases their receipts and leaves a surplus. There are many reasons why overseas government spending increases: the cost of running embassies abroad, trade promotion and foreign aid all tend to creep up, in accordance with Parkinson's Law. But by far the most usual reason for a rise in overseas spending is a foreign war or the stationing of troops on foreign soil. If the fighting is on a country's own territory (as in the Arab-Israeli conflict) the drain is limited to overseas purchases of arms and related goods. But if a country is fighting on the other side of the world, such as the Americans in Vietnam, the cost in foreign exchange soars. Not only does it have to pay for local supplies, but much of the money it pays its troops will be spent overseas in foreign currency. Even the stationing of troops abroad, such as British troops in Germany, parts of the Middle East and Far East, has the same effect on the balance of payments.

The final reason why a country's balance of payments may go into deficit is not concerned with trade (invisible or visible) nor with government expenditure: a country can also face a capital deficit when it invests overseas more than it can afford. Deficits on capital account are of a different order to trade 'losses'. The country making the investment gains an asset and in theory can always sell it off again if it cannot afford to pay for it. Furthermore the investment should provide an income, so ultimately (if the investment is profitable) it will pay for itself. But the country still has to find money to pay for the investment, which will thus become a drain on the country's reserves. So in the short run a deficit arising from investments abroad will undermine a country's accounts, unless it is offset by corresponding investment in the country itself by foreigners. This kind of investment can also be short-term, but in this case it can also reflect a lack of confidence in the country's currency.

So much for the theoretical framework. How does the experience of the United Kingdom and the United States fit in? Are their balance of payments records really as bad as they seem at first glance? Britain's overseas payments for the years 1964 to 1968 are set out in Table I. The three sections we have

Table I: *How Britain's Foreign Payments are made up*

(£ millions)	1966	1967	1968
Payments for Imports	5,211	5,574	6,801
Receipts from Exports	5,108	5,026	6,103
A. Total Visible Transactions	−103	−548	−698
Payments for Services* to foreigners	2,051	2,160	2,506
Payments from Services* to foreigners	2,832	3,081	3,615
B. Total Private Invisible Transactions	+781	+921	+1,109
C. Total Government Transactions	−633	−638	−697
Total Current Payments (A + B + C)	+64	−238	−265

Note: A plus sign indicates money owed to Britain, while a minus sign indicates money owed by Britain.

* Including 'interest, profits and dividends' and transfers.

been describing—invisible trade, invisible services and government transactions—are set out on the lines A, B and C. As will be seen there was only one overall payments surplus out of the three years. The rest were in deficit. But these deficits were made up in a significant way. In the first place visible trade produced *deficits* in every year without exception and invisible services produced *surpluses* in every year again without exception. Secondly, government spending abroad (on the upkeep of embassies, on foreign aid and on defence commitments) produced extremely high deficits. This pattern had been familiar for a number of years, but it is only in the last decade and a half that government spending abroad has produced such large deficits. The pattern of deficits on visible trade and surpluses on invisible is much more historical. In the last 180 years there have been only seven recorded surpluses on visible trade: in 1797, 1802, 1816, 1821, 1822, 1956 and 1958. Over the same extended period, invisible services have produced a persistent surplus, enough in virtually every year to cover the visible deficit. Government spending, however, has no such lengthy historical record. It emerged as a payments item between the two world wars but remained negligible. After the war spending rarely exceeded £100 million in any year until the mid-1950s. From then on it rose persistently until it exceeded £400 million in 1964.

Thus, without going into any deep analysis, two reasons can be adduced for Britain's almost persistent payments deficit in the middle 1960s. One was the rise in government spending abroad. The other was the widening of the visible trade gap. The trade balance of any country fluctuates from year to year (this is one of the main reasons why countries need reserves in the first place). But if the worst years since the war (1955, 1960 and 1964) are analysed the trade gap is seen to have risen from £313 million, to £406 million, then to £537 million. The main reason for the move into overall surplus in 1969 was a dramatic narrowing of the visible trade gap, coupled with a rise in the invisible surplus.

The United States figures have shown quite a different pattern to those of the UK. Instead of a trading deficit, until 1968 there was a substantial trade surplus. To this had to be added a further surplus on invisible account. But these were more than wiped out by massive US government expenditure and private investment overseas. Some (very) round figures will

35

quickly demonstrate this. During the 1950s and for most of the 1960s there was a visible trade surplus running at over $3,000 million a year (in 1964 it was $6,000 million). On top of this there was a further surplus of $1,500 million on invisible account making a total surplus of at least $4,500 million available for investment and government expenditure abroad. But net investment overseas was taking $2,000 million to $5,000 million a year, and the government was spending at least a further $5,000 million, leaving a deficit of $2,000 million to $3,000 million and more. These are very round figures, but they give some idea of the broad situation up to 1967: the US was only in deficit because its industry chose to invest as much money as it did overseas, and because its government had massive aid and military expenditure commitments.

One final question may now be puzzling the reader—if both the United States and the United Kingdom have been running deficits, on and off since the war, how have they managed to pay for them? To some extent they have used their gold reserves; to some extent they have paid in other currencies they have earned earlier; to some extent they have borrowed from other nations and institutions; and to some extent they have found other countries willing to hold their own currencies—pounds and dollars—in large amounts. This last method of payment is highly significant and we shall explain why these currencies have had this special treatment—and why they have been regarded and used as 'reserve currencies'—in the next chapter.

Chapter 4

WHICH CURRENCIES ARE STRONGER?

Now that London is the clearing house to foreign countries, London has a new liability to foreign countries. At whatever place many people have to make payments, at that place those people must keep money. A large deposit of foreign money in London is now necessary for the business of the world.
     Walter Bagehot, *Lombard Street*, 1873.

We have heard a lot in recent years about the special roles played by dollars and pounds in world trade. Are these roles a benefit or a burden to Britain and America? How hard would the City of London be hit by a decline in the international importance of the pound? Would the whole international money system collapse if either currency were in some way to be withdrawn from this position? It is not hard to understand why such questions are asked: the use of the pound and dollar in international payments has been at the very core of our world money system since the war. Our aim in this chapter, therefore, is to set out what this world role is: how pounds and dollars have come to be used to a far greater extent than other currencies; and how it was that pounds and dollars, rather than say Swiss francs, found themselves lumbered with the function of keeping world trade on the move.

Unfortunately, just to make things more confusing, this so-called world role is really two quite separate functions. We have already explained how payments are made between countries, and how this differs from the individual bills that have to be settled between traders. Sterling and dollars are used at both these levels, and when people talk about world roles, they are often not very explicit about which function they are referring to. In fact pounds and dollars are used both by governments and by private traders. Even if sterling were to be taken out of other countries' official reserves (and replaced perhaps with some true international currency) one might still find that international trade was dependent on it.

These two functions are what economists call their 'reserve currency' role and their 'trading currency' role. But before we try to explain the difference more fully, it is worth considering for a moment why one currency seems to be more acceptable (or favoured) than another. Basically it is not much different from the question of why one commodity is used as money rather than another: the answer invariably concerns security and convenience. People and countries will use and (more important) hold currencies they can trust and find convenient. Let us look at a concrete example.

Rather than take the reader to the desert island so beloved of the economists, come instead to Looney's Bar in Ireland. The following extract from an article by Lord Kilbracken[1] describes what happened when the Irish banks closed for three months in the summer of 1966.

'The handsome yellow doors of the one-and-only bank here will open on Friday for the first time in three long months. The strike of bank officials, settled in Northern Ireland some weeks ago, has at last ended in the Republic too. And the crunch has come for a nation that has been living on tick, willynilly, since May.

'Killeshandra, my nearest village, is where I have my banking account. Not till those yellow doors were closed did I come to realize the bank's importance and convenience. . . .

'The first thing that happened was that most grocers and almost all pubs became bankers overnight. They were taking lots of money which they didn't like keeping in cash.

'So they were happy to change cheques much more readily than usual. They also made many arrangements with local factories and offices which took no cash but required it for wages.

[1] The *Evening Standard* (London), August 1966.

'The money taken across the counter at Looney's Bar was sent down the road to pay the wages at O'Rourke's factory.

'Then things went a stage further. Looney would receive in return O'Rourke's unencashable cheque. But the credit standing of Seamus O'Rourke is good, and it would be accepted by the wholesaler in payment of Looney's account.

'The wholesaler, in turn, would pass it on, till eventually it might find its way back to Seamus, who could happily tear it up.'

The point is that people found it convenient to use Seamus O'Rourke's cheques as money since they were found to be acceptable; they were also happy to hold them presumably because O'Rourke's factory was working well and its credit was good. Much the same thing happens to international currencies. Instead of cashing sterling cheques (or their equivalent) immediately with an English bank, traders discovered that other people and nations would accept such credits (the equivalent of O'Rourke's cheques) quite happily. Since pounds, therefore, were readily acceptable in payment by most other nations, since they could be used to insure, ship and finance trade through London and since, above all, they could be invested overnight in London at a useful rate of interest, the habit grew up of using and holding pounds rather than cashing them in at the Bank of England. It is in this fashion that a *potential* world currency is born.

We mentioned earlier that there were two roles carried out by pounds and dollars: as *trading* currencies and as *reserve* currencies. As we explained this is really a distinction between the use of a currency by an individual trader and its use by a government or government agency. Usually the trader will wish to use it to settle his debts; while governments will tend to hold it as a store of value. If we trace the historical development of the world roles of sterling, this distinction should become clearer. The emergence of sterling as a world currency is easily traceable to the nineteenth-century gold standard. It can in fact be argued that the reason the gold standard worked so well was that it was in reality a sterling standard. Gold provided a

39

measure of value, but sterling helped to settle and finance trade.

A special set of factors had come together in Britain in the second half of the last century. Foremost among these was Britain's leading position both as a trading nation and as an exporter of capital. Britain's increasing exports and imports had to be financed and the so-called bill on London[1] was developed by the accepting houses (that is the merchant banks) as the most convenient mechanism for doing so. In fact it was so convenient that it was adopted by much of the rest of the world. Thus the principle of using sterling and the London banking mechanism to finance trade was gradually established. And where payments were made, working balances were kept too. Equally, as Britain was lending her surplus savings overseas, other countries also got into the habit of borrowing sterling to finance their capital investment. Since these countries had a continuing demand for pounds for international settlements (and since pounds were immediately exchangeable for gold) it is not surprising that by the end of the century many of them, such as India, had begun to hold a small part of their reserves in pounds. Thus by the First World War the trading function of sterling was well established and the reserve role was already appearing in embryonic form.

The nineteenth-century gold standard was brought to an abrupt end by the First World War. But from the point of view of sterling's international role the war had one striking effect— Britain's short-term debts were vastly increased. In order to pay for the war, the country was forced to sell off many of her investments overseas and beyond this also accumulated a pile of short-term liabilities. As a result an increased stock of pounds ended up in foreign hands. Here again were the beginnings of a potential reserve currency.

It was, however, between the two world wars that the real

[1] A bill of exchange was (and still is) a promise to pay a given sum on a given date and is normally provided, say, by a foreign importer, while awaiting the shipment of goods. These bills were 'accepted' by London's merchant banks, that is, they guaranteed payment on the due date, in return for a commission. As a result of their name appearing on the bill, the bills could be discounted in the money market, and thus the holders of the bills (usually the exporters) could get cash immediately, less the appropriate discount or rate of interest.

foundations for the use of the pound as a world *reserve* currency were laid. As the world plunged into economic depression and as currency crises proliferated from 1929 onwards, defensive currency blocs began to emerge.[1] One was made up of a group of countries with close economic ties with Britain—the sterling bloc, later to be known as the 'Scheduled Territories' or sterling area. When the pound left the gold standard in September 1931,[2] these countries had to decide whether to continue to maintain their exchange rates at a stable rate with the pound (and to maintain their sterling reserves), or whether to stick close to gold. Those choosing the former became the sterling bloc. When war broke out in 1939, and brought with it the necessity to introduce exchange regulations to control payments between countries, both to protect the central reserves in London and to pay for the war, most of the sterling bloc became more formally linked in what became known as the sterling area. In effect they agreed on a common exchange policy for pooling their combined reserves.

During the Second World War itself even larger amounts of sterling accumulated in overseas hands. Britain was again forced to sell off some of her investments and to borrow abroad. This 'borrowing' took several forms. One was in the form of 'Lend-Lease'[3] from the United States. Another flowed naturally from the workings of the sterling area. These were such that the members, particularly those belonging to the Commonwealth, were willing to accept sterling in exchange for the delivery of goods and services to Britain. To them it was simply a matter of adding further sterling to their existing sterling reserves. To Britain it was an important method of war finance. In this way British IOUs were accepted to a total of some £3,000 million during the course of the war. India, Egypt, parts of West Africa, as well as Australia, New Zealand and South Africa, were the main recipients. These IOUs (or sterling

---

[1] More details on the growth of currency blocs in Chapter 12.

[2] See Chapter 10.

[3] An agreement between Britain and the US under which both countries supplied each other on credit. By the end of the war the balance was heavily one way. The net credit to Britain reached $23,000m.

balances) were to form a major part of the sterling area structure (and of Britain's economic problem) after the war.

All these sterling-bloc arrangements, throughout the 1930s and 1940s, were essentially defensive. It suited all members to stick together and, while encouraging the free movement of money among themselves, to erect what in effect was a trade and monetary barrier against the rest of the world. This defensive attitude continued after the war, and was formalized in 1947 when the so-called Scheduled Territories (the official name for members of the sterling area) were introduced. They agreed to introduce a common form of exchange control that is, to regulate the way in which individuals and traders could spend their money abroad so that the reserves of the different countries were protected. In effect Britain and the sterling area members made an informal bargain along the following lines:

1. Most overseas members (i.e. countries other than Britain) agreed to hold most of their reserves in sterling. This meant that they handed over dollar and other hard-currency[1] earnings to Britain in exchange for pounds. They also agreed to use sterling in their payments with the rest of the world.
2. Britain agreed to impose no restrictions on the movement of money from Britain to the sterling area.
3. Britain agreed to supply dollars and other currencies to other sterling area members in exchange for their sterling, as and when needed.
4. Britain promised sterling area members priority in borrowing on the London capital market.

In the early post-war world this suited everyone. Britain's gold reserves received the benefit of the dollar and other earnings of the other sterling area countries. These countries in turn got special treatment in borrowing from London. All members were in effect conserving their total reserves.

We have made this brief excursion of 150 to 200 years,

[1] 'Hard currency' is another phrase for strong currency: in other words a currency that is in demand (and thus useful) because everyone has faith in it.

covering the developments of the sterling area, for a simple reason: to try to explain why other countries and other countries' traders found it in their interests to hold pounds. For this in essence was how sterling's two world roles emerged. Traders found that they needed, and could benefit from, working balances in London. Some governments found that it suited them to be part of a system which allowed them to dip into London's gold reserves and to hold their own reserves in sterling. Both found it profitable to earn interest on their sterling balances: whether it equally suited, or now suits, Britain to be part of such a system is a matter we shall turn to later in this chapter.

The development of the dollar as an international currency came rather later than that of the pound. For one thing the American economy was not as dependent on international trade as Britain's. For another, the United States did not have war debts to add to the amount of its currency in foreign hands. Even so dollars were beginning to be held abroad and to be used to finance and settle international trade from the end of the First World War onwards. European traders and bankers found it convenient to do so. And so did governments. Thus by the 1920s the dollar was already sharing some of the work of an international currency with the pound. New York was rivalling London as a world financial centre. The growing size of American imports and exports and the flow of American capital abroad all led to the use of the dollar as a world trading currency. By the 1930s, it has been estimated, pounds and dollars were sharing eighty per cent of this world role between them.

The dollar's role as a *reserve* currency was (very much like sterling's) a later development. But its use in this role had a different origin. When the United States finally devalued in 1934, the dollar, in contrast to the pound, did not sever its link with gold. A new rate of $35 to the ounce was established but, more important, the Secretary of the US Treasury announced that the US would be willing to *buy* gold at this price and to release it at about the same price to certain central banks. It was this commitment, making the dollar 'as good as gold',

43

that was to play such a vital role in the immediate post-war world, when the dollar became the only direct currency link with gold and, for that reason, as well as its growing use as a world trading currency, an alternative to gold in many countries' reserves.

It is time to see how far these changes in the use of pounds and dollars have been reflected in the world's monetary reserves. The following figures show clearly how the roles of the pound and the dollar have been reversed since the war:

	Gold $000	% of Total	Sterling $000	% of Total	Dollars $000	% of Total	Total
1937*	26·0	86	2·3	8	1·8	6	30·0
1952	34·3	72	7·5	16	5·7	12	47·5
1963	39·2	67	6·8	12	11·9	21	57·4

* Estimates.

While the share of gold in the world's reserves has been declining, the persistent rise in the use of the dollar is striking. Since the 1950s the United States has been running an almost continuous overall deficit on her balance of payments—mainly reflecting her heavy investment overseas and her expenditure on aid and defence. As a result more dollars have been earned abroad and the amount of dollars held abroad has been rising. Between 1963 (as shown above) and 1967 when they reached a peak, dollar liabilities abroad rose further from nearly $12,000 million to over $18,000 million.

The dollar has been replacing, or at least overtaking, the pound in settling international trade too. For a time, after the war, it was estimated that sterling financed or helped to settle close on 50 per cent of world trade. By 1960 this had dropped to around 35 per cent and by 1965 it was probably between 25 and 30 per cent. The equivalent percentage for the dollar must have reached at least 35 per cent—thus surpassing the pound—over the same period.

In this account of the world's reserves the reader will have noted that two particular reasons led to the rising share made up of pounds and dollars. One was the large deficits and thus

44

debts, incurred by Britain in paying for the war; and the other was the continuous deficits incurred by the United States over the past decade and a half in fulfilment of her world political role. This immediately highlights one of the major dilemmas facing the world's finance ministers. The less successful Britain and the United States are in keeping their payments in balance, the more pounds and dollars become available through their deficits to lubricate world trade. At the same time the continuing deficits will in themselves undermine confidence in these two currencies. On the other hand, the more successful Britain and the United States are in balancing their payments the stronger their currencies but the fewer pounds and dollars will be available. Little wonder that many people, besides General de Gaulle, have concluded that there must be a better way to finance world trade than leaving the supply of the world's reserves and finance to the ups and downs in the payments of two particular countries. We shall have more to say about this particular argument later when we explore the future alternatives to the present monetary system.

For the moment we must confine our comments to the effect of this so-called gold exchange system on Britain and the United States. The immediate benefit to any country whose currency is held rather than immediately presented for payment (say, into gold) is that the country is, in effect, being given a credit. In the case of the United States, for example, many foreign countries have been happy to hold dollars rather than ask for gold. Jacques Rueff, the distinguished French economist and one of de Gaulle's financial advisers, once commented that this process reduced the world monetary system 'to a mere children's game in which one party has agreed to give back their investments, after each game of marbles, to the party who had lost the game'. However one looks at it, at a time when dollars have been ending up in foreign hands because of a deficit in American payments (this has been largely true for the past fifteen years), the United States has been able to conserve its gold reserves more than it might otherwise have done and, to that extent, has been given more time to put its economy in order. This, according to its critics, has enabled the US to do

45

four things: to run a deficit without the normal disciplines affecting other countries; to gain flexibility on domestic policy; to acquire larger holdings in foreign industry than it could otherwise have done; and to export inflation to other nations. Not all these charges are fully accepted by economists, but they illustrate the feeling that, in some way, the present system is allowing the United States and, to a lesser degree, Britain greater freedom than other countries can obtain. These charges must not, however, blind us to the fact that costs are involved in running world currencies too. Holders of dollars or pounds are not necessarily firm holders. They have always had the option of changing their mind and deciding to take gold rather than hold the chosen currency, depending on their current assessment of it. This possibility has been a threat to virtually every British government since the war and has plainly led to restrictive economic policies and, in the view of some observers, has continually curbed the natural growth of the British economy.

To sum up, there are both benefits and costs attaching to the operation of a world currency, and they can change over time. One economist, Mr Sidney Rolfe, summed up American post-war experience in this way: 'Until about 1958 the United States enjoyed the benefits. Other nations were happy to acquire dollar holdings and the American position was thought to be impregnable. However, since 1958, because the US deficits have continued to run at higher levels, and due to the convertibility of European currencies, the United States has faced the costs.' Some would argue that Britain has been paying the costs for far longer.

Chapter 5

WHY EXCHANGE RATES VARY

*. . . We must endeavour at all costs not to be led away by
the notion that depreciation of the currency is a short cut
to prosperity which can be taken without expense to anyone, or, still less, taken again and again.*

So said *The Economist*, after a devaluation of sterling, not in
1967, nor indeed in 1949, but way back in 1931. Since it has
often been suggested that the only way Britain can hope to
match the economic growth of the rest of the developed world is
by constantly depreciating her currency, such thoughts have
become very relevant again. The task of this chapter is to sort
out how exchange rates between currencies are changed, the
differences between so-called 'fixed' and 'floating' rates, and
what happens when a country devalues its currency. But before
we start, it is worth going back for a moment to the position we
reached in Chapter 2, when we were talking about the foreign
exchange market, and considering again what factors determine
the prices the foreign exchange brokers are shouting amid the
hubbub of the dealers' room.

In the first instance, of course, the main factor is the amount
of pounds, dollars, or whatever the bank needs to buy or sell.
The dealer in London may have an order to buy a certain
number of dollars for one of his bank's customer's. His job is to
get them at the best possible price. But if the thousands of
individual deals are added together it is unlikely that the amount
of pounds and dollars on offer will match exactly and the price
will have to move to even up the difference. In other words the
foreign exchange market is, in principle, just the same as a
cattle or corn market.

Ultimately the shortage or surplus of a country's currency
that appears on the foreign exchange market is dependent on its
overall balance of payments position, as well as on the amount

47

of its currency already held by foreigners. Thus, in the case of Britain, the volume of pounds being offered in the exchange market can be the result of holders of existing sterling balances deciding to sell or it can be a simple reflection of the state of Britain's current payments. This was why, in July 1957, Britain found large amounts of pounds being sold in the exchange market, in spite of running a surplus on her current payments. Holders of pounds can lose confidence in their future value even when payments are still in surplus. We have already explained how deficits and surpluses arise, and it is not hard to go on from there to see that if a country has an overall deficit (i.e. with all the other countries put together) its currency will tend to fall in price. It is also not difficult to understand that holders of sterling can push the price down too. Whether or not the price (or exchange rate) will be allowed to move depends on the system of exchange rates in operation.

There are two main systems—'fixed' rates and 'floating' rates—and a number of variations in between them. Since the last war we have been using a fixed-rate system governed by rules introduced at the Bretton Woods Conference of 1944, and supported by the International Monetary Fund, which was set up by the Conference. Under this arrangement the governments of the countries involved (effectively everybody except the Communist bloc) have undertaken to maintain their exchange rates at an agreed level, or parity, and are only permitted to alter them in the case of what is described as 'fundamental disequilibrium', though just what constitutes such an eventuality is not fully spelt out. These parities are agreed in relation to gold or the US dollar. The dollar itself is fixed in relation to gold only (i.e. at $35 an ounce).

It will already be apparent that even the 'fixed'-rate system has a certain limited flexibility about it. In the first place the agreed rate is adjustable occasionally, that is, a currency can be devalued[1] against other currencies, particularly when it is recognized that a country's price level has got out of line with (usually risen above) those in other countries. Devaluation of

---

[1] It can also be revalued, that is *raised* in value in relation to other currencies as the German mark was in 1961, and again in 1969.

the pound, for example, means that in future more pounds have to be offered for dollars and other currencies. There is also another way in which exchange rates are not rigid. Exchange rates between currencies are only kept close to the agreed parities, not spot on them. Under IMF rules exchange rates can move on either side of the agreed parity up to a maximum of 1 per cent on each side. For example, the margin for the sterling/dollar rate of $2.40 is $2.38 to $2.42 dollars to the pound. But in practice central banks (like the Bank of England) usually choose narrower limits than this. If the rate in the exchange market falls to the bottom limit set by the central bank it is obliged to step in and check the movement by buying its own currency. Although dollars are in practice used for this purpose, central banks are in effect using their gold and exchange reserves. Conversely, if the rate tries to rise above the top limit, the central bank must sell its own currency to pull the rate back. In practice a central bank usually intervenes through chosen commercial banks or occasionally through other central banks, the main aim being to check movements long before they reach even the narrow limits set down. It is this kind of operation that the newspapers are describing when they speak of the Bank of England 'supporting the pound'. In these circumstances so many pounds are being offered by foreign holders in the market that the Bank is forced to buy them, with dollars or gold, to prevent the sterling rate from moving outside the agreed limits (in this case below the lower level of $2.38).

To see why this particular system of fixed exchange rates was chosen at Bretton Woods in 1944 we have to glance back briefly at the period between the wars. Pre-war experience clearly set the minds of the men of Bretton Woods firmly against three things: the competitive currency devaluations of the 1930s in which each country had tried to gain a trade advantage over its rivals by depreciating its currency faster than them, and thus stimulating its own exports at the expense of others; the chaos that had resulted from floating exchange rates; and the restrictions on both trade and movements of capital. The 1944 monetary conference, therefore, decided on two things; not only must exchange rates be held steady, but countries must be helped to hold them steady. Out of this second decision came the International Monetary Fund itself.

In the years since the war the system has not worked too badly. There has been no repetition of the calamities of the 1930s and the world has experienced an unprecedented expansion both in trade and prosperity. Nevertheless currency crises have occurred with ever-increasing regularity since the beginning of the 1960s: and two particular problems have faced the world's finance ministers. One is whether there is enough world money ('liquidity' in the current jargon) to finance a continued expansion in world trade. The other is the apparent difficulty of changing exchange rate parities in a smooth and logical manner. Although, as we shall see, some economists believe that the two problems are closely linked, for the moment we want to concentrate on the exchange rate adjustment problem.

There are a number of reasons why the fixed-rate system of the Bretton Woods agreement has led to instability. We have already stressed that the foreign exchange market is like any other market; that the price for the various currencies depends on the supply and demand for them. We have also pointed out that any country running a balance of payments deficit will tend to find its exchange rate slipping. Because of the deficit, which puts more of its currency into foreign hands, more people will want to sell the currency than to buy it.

A deficit, however, is not the only way pressure can build up against a currency. It may also face speculative pressures—that is, foreigners may be persuaded to sell currency holdings they have had for some time—and these are pressures to which the fixed-rate system is particularly prone. When the exchange rate of a country is for some reason suspect—most usually because its value is thought to be too high—banks, companies and some private individuals may start to speculate against it. Despite the emotive tone of this word—the idea of hard-faced men at their Zürich desks growling 'sell sterling' into telephones—the process is simple and, within the framework of our monetary system, perfectly legitimate. This is how it works.

Suppose there is a feeling that sterling is overpriced in relation to other currencies. We need not go into the reasons for

50

this: it may be because of a persistent balance of payments deficit; it may be because of rapidly rising prices which, it is feared, will make her exports uncompetitive; or it may be because of general monetary uncertainties not directly connected with the position of the British balance of payments. The important thing is that people think the rate may be forced to move from the present $2.40 to, say, $2.00. If this happened they would obviously make a loss on any pounds they held. Therefore they make efforts to protect their interests by selling their holdings before the decline takes place. Others, of course, may wish to sell sterling in the hope of buying it back later at a cheaper exchange rate.

In the early post-war years these kind of pressures on currencies were much smaller than they have been in recent years. The reason was that it was not as easy to switch out of one currency into another—only the dollar was freely convertible into gold or other currencies. From the end of 1958 onwards, however, the major European currencies (including the pound) also became freely convertible and holders of foreign funds were able to switch them from one centre to another as it suited them. The rate of interest in each centre became increasingly important in influencing these movements. One result was that large masses of short-term capital could move into and out of a currency almost overnight. Thus the speculative attack on a suspect currency could be far larger than ever before.

The trouble was that these increased pressures were building up against a particularly rigid system of exchange rates. Although the monetary experts at Bretton Woods had assumed that a currency would be devalued once a 'fundamental disequilibrium' existed between it and other currencies, no precise definition was offered: nor was any procedure laid down for changing an exchange rate, beyond so-called 'consultations' with the International Monetary Fund. And as time went on, prestige began to attach itself to existing exchange rates and governments felt it to be a matter of pride to stick to a rate even though its maintenance could only mean unnecessarily restrictive policies at home. Thus pride and political prestige too often prevented sensible and timely adjustments, as the world saw all

51

too clearly in the winter of 1968–9 when President de Gaulle prevented a devaluation of the franc virtually single-handed.

We might pause for a moment at this point to sum up the difficulties faced with the post-war system of exchange rates. In the first place no easy method of changing a rate has been worked out. Secondly, governments have resisted such changes, sometimes up to the last moment, because of national pride or prestige. Thirdly, the need for more frequent changes (certainly for more flexibility) has arisen from the contrasts in domestic policies pursued by different countries. Fourthly, the growing freedom for the movement of capital across frontiers has placed additional strains on the fixed-rate system.

This partly explains why devaluations have so often become such apparently earth-shattering events. But we must now explore what such moves actually mean.

Devaluation of a currency is the most drastic adjustment possible in a system of fixed exchange rates. The new rate is usually expressed in terms of gold but its practical effect is to change the value of one currency in terms of all others. When sterling was devalued in November 1967, it meant that afterwards a British resident was able to exchange a pound note for only $2.40 compared with $2.80 previously. Such a change means, of course, that the country devaluing its currency is able to offer its goods for export at a cheaper rate *in terms of its own currency* than was previously possible. In the case of imports the opposite is true. Residents find that the cost of foreign goods, again *in terms of their own currency*, has gone up. Thus devaluation, by making exports cheaper and imports more expensive, is intended to bring a better balance into a country's overseas payments by stimulating exports and curbing imports. There is one snag, of course. Devaluation is not only a built-in regulator of a payments deficit. It is also a recognition that a country's living standards have become too high in relation to its productivity: its price-levels have got out of line with those of other countries. And devaluation is deliberately intended to adjust internal conditions accordingly, that is, to lower living standards by raising prices.

In other words devaluation is usually brought on by a significant widening of a country's visible trade gap. This was one of the factors in Britain's devaluation in 1967. In that year, partly because of a damaging dock strike and partly for other more fundamental reasons, Britain's visible trade gap reached £635 million (compared with only £136 million in 1966). But there were other factors at work too, and it is important to realize that devaluation can have several causes. For one thing the Government's overseas commitments were producing an annual deficit of between £400 million and £500 million. As we explained earlier, this expenditure went on defence overseas, on aid to underdeveloped countries and on such things as the upkeep of embassies, etc. For another thing Britain continued to export private capital on a significant scale. Above all, there was a widespread lack of confidence, not only in the pound itself but in the Government and its ability to run affairs generally. This could be expressed directly because of the large amounts of sterling held abroad. Holders began to sell a growing volume in the early part of November 1967. And added to this were such things as 'leads and lags' on normal commercial payments. We shall explain these in more detail later, but briefly they are deliberate changes in the timing of payments in order to avoid a currency loss. British importers can advance their payments and foreign buyers can delay theirs. The former are trying to avoid paying more later while the latter are hoping to get things cheaper by waiting. Such legitimate actions can have a large impact on the central gold reserves. It is estimated, for example, that if all sterling area import payments are made one week earlier it will cost the reserves £150 million.

To sum up, we have put our finger on at least four possible causes of the sterling devaluation of 1967: the widening visible trade gap; the size of the Government's expenditure overseas; excessive private investment overseas; and a basic loss of confidence (and hence sales) by foreign holders of sterling. The reader can take his choice or perhaps (wisely) conclude that all were contributing factors.

Whatever the prime cause, sterling's 1967 devaluation had one result; it left the world's exchange markets more nervous than it found them. Soon there was a rush into gold, then a rush out of

53

French francs and into Deutschmarks. And throughout this period the world's finance ministers demonstrated how difficult it was to readjust currency parities. It was not long before there were calls for greater flexibility in exchange rates and it was only a short step from this to the vocal arguments (from Professor Milton Friedman and others) for the re-introduction of floating rates to resolve most of the world's monetary ailments. Leading economists began to advocate floating rates as the only alternative to the illogicalities of the existing system.

The principle behind floating rates is simple. When pressures build up against a currency (that is when more people wish to sell it than to buy it) and the exchange rate automatically moves downwards, it is allowed to do so. In theory, therefore, no reserves are needed to control the rate. The rate itself will then begin to adjust the economy both gradually and automatically. The gradual fall in the rate will lower export prices and raise import prices. Such a system, it is claimed, will decide the true worth of a currency just as any free market does for goods in general. It will also avoid the build-up of speculative pressures so often encouraged by the fixed-rate system. And since adjustments between different economies would be going on all the time as exchange rates fluctuated against each other, it is argued that governments could pursue domestic policies (whether inflationary or deflationary) without affecting each other as directly as they do when exchange rates are fixed. This, it is strongly suggested, would provide governments with far more autonomy over economic policies, monetary or fiscal, than they have at present.

One further argument is marshalled on the side of floating rates. It is suggested that flexible exchange rates might go far towards curing the apparent shortage of 'international liquidity', that is of world money to finance international trade. If, for example, a deficit appears in a country's payments, when fixed rates are in operation, the country will need exchange reserves (international liquidity) to defend the rate or to prevent the rate from slipping. If the currency in question was on a floating rate, the rate would depreciate and no corresponding reserves would be needed.

54

On the other hand several difficulties are cited against floating rates. One is that it makes it difficult for traders. Because of daily, even hourly fluctuations, they cannot know exactly what price they are trading at, unless the customer buys the necessary currency on what is known as the *forward market*[1] at the same time as he placed his order. More important, and the main reason why some bankers hate it, a floating rate robs the Government's economic policies of any discipline and could conceivably increase the risk of a collapse of the currency. When put in an international context these dangers become more apparent. If all rates were free to fluctuate, a government making a mistake in its stabilization policy by inflating a little fast might simply bring about a decline in the value of its currency. But in contrast to the fixed-rate system there would be no disciplines—such as an immediate decline in reserves—to persuade a government to introduce restrictive measures.

Even if governments did resist the temptation to over-inflate, there would be other dangers. Speculators might continue to sell a depreciating currency in the expectation that it would fall still further. A country with a depreciating currency might find that it could not build up its exports fast enough to stabilize it at the correct long-term level; the breathing space that a country needs to sort out its trade position after a devaluation would not exist.

So much for the theoretical arguments. What can we learn from pre- or post-war experience? Before the war the pound was on a flexible basis from 1931 onwards, with occasional interventions by the authorities to smooth out excessive fluctuations especially after 1934. Many people regard it as a modestly successful experiment in that it enabled Britain to stage an economic recovery during the 1930s. But other countries were on floating rates too and, it is still strongly argued, the resultant continued depreciation of currencies did more than anything else to undermine the international monetary system in that period. Since the war Mexico, Peru, Lebanon,

[1] A 'forward' market can relate to rubber, tea, tin or any commodity as well as currencies. It is a market in which the delivery or promise of delivery of commodities (or currencies) one month, two, months or say, six months ahead can be traded in. Technically, its purpose is to afford some protection against the future fluctuation in the price of a commodity or a currency.

Syria and Thailand have all experimented with flexible rates. But the most important currency to operate on a floating-rate basis has been the Canadian dollar. Canada had a fluctuating rate between September 1950 and May 1962. It was originally introduced in an effort to reduce a heavy inflow of capital from the United States. Its main effect, looking back, was to dampen down the Canadian economy. By the end of the period unemployment had reached a peak of over 7 per cent and Canada's share of world exports had dropped from nearly 6 per cent to a little over 4 per cent.

The fact was that throughout this period Canada had a continuing payments deficit which naturally inhibited domestic economic policy. But the exchange rate was prevented from moving down (which would have given the necessary stimulus to exports and thus to the economy as a whole) by a continuous inflow of capital. In part this was long-term investment capital from the United States, but a large volume of short-term money was also attracted because Canadian interest rates were higher than those in the us. In short a speculative movement largely offset the normal economic forces which would have been produced by the exchange rate. It can be argued that the inflow of capital could have been avoided had the Canadian authorities forced down interest rates to below those in the us. But the point remains that a floating rate is not enough in itself to ensure that all goes well with an economy. It may even increase a country's dependence on external influences.

But if, as these practical results seem to suggest, the floating-rate system also has its faults, what other alternatives are there?

There are two main such compromise candidates. Firstly, the present system could be modified by widening the bands within which currencies are allowed to move: instead of 1 per cent either way, this could be widened to say 5 per cent. This was advocated by Lord Keynes way back in 1930, and the British Treasury and Bank of England are said to have given the idea their tentative approval in the early 1950s. But there are many objections. It has never been tried. It is not clear whether it would increase or decrease speculative pressure. Once a currency reached one end of the band, all the problems of a fixed rate would appear. Trade might be made difficult if the range of fluctuation was too great. And the fundamental problem of what would happen when a country had to move beyond the range of the limits would remain unsolved.

With all these difficulties, it is not surprising that interest has shifted to another 'half-way house'—the most esoteric of the exchange rate systems, the 'crawling peg'. This is another variation on the present system. In most versions the currencies would be allowed to fluctuate between small margins, as at present. The point is that these margins (or 'pegs') would be allowed to fluctuate very slightly (to 'crawl'), whereas at present they can only be changed in the case of 'fundamental dis-equilibrium'. They would be permitted to move by very small amounts, weekly, monthly, perhaps even daily. The movement would be based on the average of rates in the immediate past. The total movement during a year would be restricted to perhaps 2 per cent.

The advantages claimed for the 'crawling peg' are that it would combine the certainty of the present system with the need for a more flexible adjustment mechanism. It would probably be compatible with the present rules of the IMF, and it would avoid the kind of worldwide inflation that the floating system might possibly engender. But it has never been tried.

Chapter 6

THE ART OF AVOIDING CRISES

The International Monetary Conference has agreed to the
following principles; standard currency is to be gold, the
smallest gold coin to be a five-franc piece, all other gold
pieces to be a multiple of five. The monetary uniformity to
be based upon the French standard, silver coin only to
serve for change: the coin of each State to pass current in
the other States.
—*The Times*, July 8, 1867.

The history of international monetary help goes back a long
way. The first known operation of this kind is said to have been
in 1838, when the Bank of England drew credits on Paris by
arrangement with the Bank of France, for over £400,000. True
to present-day standards of reticence, the government did not
publicly acknowledge the transactions until 1840.

Today no international operation makes as exhilarating
reading as the efforts of central banks and Treasury officials to
mobilize the millions of dollars needed to prop up a shaky
exchange rate, or fight off massive speculative attacks on an
unconvincing parity. Midnight flights of top-level officials to
Bonn, secret talks in Basle and confidential negotiations at the
OECDs[1] Chateau de la Muette in Paris all have the air of
urgency and inscrutability of an Interpol mystery thriller.

The reasons for the sense of urgency in these operations will
already have become apparent. What this chapter tries to do is
to make them a little more 'scrutable'—to explain the
immediate background to international monetary relief
operations, to set out the main channels through which help
can be given, and to try to explain how they work.

From the mid-1950s until the second half of 1968, international monetary assistance almost invariably meant help for

[1] Organization for Economic Co-operation and Development.

sterling. There were three major sterling crises in the 1960s and several minor ones. The significant upheavals were in March 1961, sparked off by the revaluation of the German Deutschmark and the Dutch guilder: in November 1964, when new Labour Party Ministers aggravated an already sensitive payments problem bequeathed to them by the outgoing Tory Government; and in November 1967 which culminated in the devaluation of the pound from $2.80 to $2.40. But other countries have received help from time to time too: France, Italy, Holland, Belgium, even the United States.

International assistance can mean several different things. It may be a formal system of loans to countries trying to right a balance of payments deficit, through channels such as the International Monetary Fund and its agency, the General Arrangement to Borrow. It may be an informal and *ad hoc* arrangement to cope with temporary flights of 'hot money' (short-term speculative funds). Or it may not take the form of a loan at all, but operate through a tax adjustment like the German 'shadow revaluation' of November 1968, which involved a higher tax on exports and a lower duty on imports, coupled with provisions to deter inflows of speculative capital. We shall explain the differences in a moment. But, basically, help is sought when decisive action is needed to allay fears that a country's reserves of gold and foreign exchange are in danger of running out or becoming rapidly depleted. Other countries agree to lend money, usually on condition that the borrowing country will take action to put right whatever caused the trouble in the first place.

There are several different reasons why a country may call for help. In the first place, some event may have touched off a sudden loss of confidence in its currency: the German revaluation of March 1961 and the statements and actions of the new Labour Ministers in Britain in October and November 1964 both affected sterling in this way. As a result private individuals decide to change their money into a currency which they believe to be safer. Exporters try to postpone payment in a foreign currency in the hope that it may become worth more, and importers hurry to pay their bills in the fear that their own

59

currency may become worth less. As everyone tries to get rid of the mistrusted currency, the central bank becomes the only buyer, exchanging a rapidly dwindling pile of foreign exchange reserves for its own unwanted money, in an effort to maintain its agreed exchange rate. When this happens, the central bank may call on other central banks to lend it fresh supplies of foreign exchange in the hope that when suspicions about the exchange rate have died away, people will begin to buy its currency again and replenish the bank's stock of foreign exchange.

This is the most frequent kind of international emergency. No satisfactory way has been invented to put an end to these sudden transfers of private money from one currency to another, apart from exchange controls. As long as crises of confidence provoke movements of 'hot money' from one centre to another, international co-operation, particularly among central banks will remain the most convenient way to deal with them.

Secondly, a country may also call on international help to support its exchange rate because its basic balance of payments is in disequilibrium. Its imports may be exceeding its exports, and causing a heavier drain on its reserves than the country can support unaided. Then its potential creditors are faced with a choice. They may feel that the imbalance is temporary and that a loan will tide the country through until balance is restored. (Developing countries that are heavily dependent on trade in one commodity may be thrown into this kind of position by a bad crop, for example.) Alternatively the creditors may feel that the deficit is the result of unsuitable domestic policies. They may grant assistance, but accompany it with formal or informal conditions or inquisitions. The International Monetary Fund requires heavy 'debtors' to submit to close surveillance as a matter of course.

Finally, the creditors may feel that the country is in a state of fundamental disequilibrium: that is the relation between its domestic structure of costs and prices and its external exchange rate is fundamentally out of balance, and that a change in the parity of its currency is the only long-term cure. Central bankers are especially loath to come to this kind of conclusion, with its inevitable implications of upheaval and disruption for the international monetary system as a whole. Even if they do, as we have seen, exchange rate changes involve a political decision and if governments refuse to play ball, even this kind of imbalance may have to be shored up with an international loan.

Thus help is given for all these reasons—largely as a stop-gap: as a temporary expedient to smooth over bumps which have arisen in the international adjustment mechanism. But, as we shall see later, there are other kinds of help (particularly from the new Special Drawing Rights scheme and the so-called 'Basle Facility') that have a more fundamental purpose. Both are intended to bring about permanent changes in the international monetary system.

Having explained briefly why international monetary help is given, it is time to explain what form it takes. The technical variety seems to be almost infinite. But, for our purpose, six different kinds stand out:

1. Nations can pool some of their gold and exchange resources in an international institution and allow it to provide help under agreed rules.
2. The central banks of individual countries (e.g. like the Bank of England, Bank of France etc.) can agree on mutual help (i.e. offering credits to each other up to an agreed amount). These are usually on a bilateral basis.
3. Central banks can decide to provide a total amount of short-term credit between them to any currency in difficulties. (This is usually a multilateral agreement.)
4. Central banks can guarantee the holdings of certain currencies against a change in its exchange rate (i.e. they may agree to compensate certain holders for such a change on certain conditions).
5. Central banks can buy or sell in the foreign exchange market and (even more important) in the forward exchange market, thereby influencing exchange rates as well as the exchange positions of individual countries.
6. Countries can agree to create a new kind of international

61

currency and to issue it in agreed amounts. (This will basically help the world economy in general but may help certain countries more than others.)

These are the main ways in which world monetary help has developed since the war. We must now try to explain how (and why) developments took the form they did. Apart from the central banks of individual countries (that is, the equivalent of the Bank of England), two institutions have been primarily involved with these operations. These need a a preliminary word of explanation, before we provide a brief outline of post-war development.

It was in the late 1920s that the first of the two major organizations now dominating international money was conceived. The Bank for International Settlements emerged against the background of the 1929 crisis. It arose out of previous *ad hoc* co-operative efforts and was set up in January 1930. It is a central bank institution, unlike the International Monetary Fund which was set up by national governments. Its shareholders include all the major free world industrial powers, as well as the Eastern European nations (though not Russia). It is certainly the only agency of international capitalism which can claim Albania as a member.

The central bankers, who gather in Basle on the second weekend of ten months of the year amid much unwelcome publicity, have been meeting there regularly since 1931, with the exception of the war years. The central bank governors who come to Basle are the directors of the BIS, and it is in that capacity that they meet there.

The International Monetary Fund, the other major organization, emerged from the Bretton Woods Conference of 1944, and was set up at the end of 1945. Like its sister institution, the World Bank, it is a 'specialized agency' of the United Nations, to which it reports, although the UN does not control its staff, membership or finances.

Both the IMF and the BIS have been at the centre of international monetary co-operation since the war. Throughout the late 1940s and the whole of the 1950s the IMF was at the forefront ; the BIS became prominent again at the beginning of the 1960s. Briefly, the role of the IMF—apart from consultation, co-operation and advice—was to provide help to countries suffering from balance of payments difficulties. It has resources amounting to some $24,000 million, subscribed by member countries who have had to provide 25 per cent of their quota in gold and the balance in their own currency. (Quotas are based on the size of members' economy, imports, etc.) Thus the Fund has a continuous stock of gold and exchange. When a member country needs help, it offers its own currency in exchange for the currency and/or gold it needs. The opposite takes place when repayments are made. A country can draw up to 25 per cent of its quota automatically and even up to 100 per cent without much difficulty, if it can show that it is taking reasonable action to solve its problems. But help beyond this point has to be justified and economic policy becomes strictly supervised, as Britain has discovered.

IMF help must be repaid within three to five years. It is also given only after discussion with the Fund's management. Until the onset of currency convertibility in Europe at the end of 1958 (as we have explained, this meant that European currencies could be automatically exchanged into any other currency), monetary pressures on individual currencies were neither swift nor massive. Afterwards, largely because of the vast amounts of international money able to cross frontiers, both the size of these movements and the swiftness with which they occurred made new kinds of monetary help essential. The turning point came in the spring of 1961. Following a strong flow of funds into gold the previous autumn largely because of growing doubts about the dollar, and immediately following the small upward revaluation of the German mark and the Dutch guilder early in 1961, nervous holders of sterling began to move into German marks, Swiss francs, French francs and Italian lire on a large scale. The normal type of IMF help proved both cumbersome and slow and eminently unsuitable for this new kind of monetary crisis. The central bank governors at their regular monthly meeting at the Bank for International Settlements in Basle quickly produced an *ad hoc* solution: a 'gentlemen's agreement' to channel the funds being invested in other currencies back to the Bank of England. Thus, instead of the Bank of England being asked to meet its obligations immediately to other central banks (mainly of Europe, and North America) by payments in gold, the evil day was put off for a further three months. A new kind of monetary help had been formulated and a new first line of defence created. Like all such devices it had its advantages as well as its dangers. It calmed down the exchange markets considerably and allowed the British Government to introduce appropriate economic measures. But, because the amount of such help is almost bound to remain a secret until well after the event, the size of the crisis can often be hidden not only from potential speculators but also from the citizens of the country whose currency is under pressure, thereby preventing sufficient corrective action because of ignorance of the true depth of the crisis.

This crisis move in Basle was the beginning of a new phase in central bank co-operation. In the eyes of some bankers the 'Basle Agreement', which was clearly the model for future co-operation, had two defects. The United States was not part of it (for special technical reasons) and it was felt that the magnitude of the potential defences ought to be more widely known if only to deter future speculation. Accordingly, the United States authorities took the initiative the following year in recommending what were to be known as 'swap arrangements' between the Federal Reserve Bank of New York and the central banks of other countries. One of the first of these 'swaps' was agreed between the Federal Reserve Bank and the Bank of England in June 1962: it was for $50 million. Soon a network of bilateral 'swaps' had been established. The idea behind them was simple. They were in essence a reciprocal credit facility. Each central bank agreed to exchange, on request, its own currency for that of other central banks up to an agreed amount for a period of three months. Thus when a currency was under pressure (that is when holders were selling it), the central bank would have need of gold or other currencies. If, for example, the pound was under pressure because holders were selling it and moving into dollars, the Bank of England would ultimately need dollars. Under its 'swap' arrangement with the Federal Reserve, the Bank of England could ask for a dollar credit for three months and would offer the equivalent amount in pounds to the Federal Reserve. They would agree to 'swap' the money back in three months' time at the same rate of exchange.

As a result of these agreements the US Federal Reserve quickly built up reciprocal arrangements to a total of $2,800 million with eleven leading central banks. By the end of 1966 they had grown to $4,500 million. They later reached $9,000 million. The period of the 'swaps' was extended to between six and twelve months. Another sizeable defence had been created.

The idea of the 'swaps' was soon accompanied by an extension of the IMFs resources. The continued series of sterling crises and the prospect that, because of the growing deficits of the United States, the dollar might soon need help from the IMF, had led to the fear that the Fund might run out of its stock of certain currencies, mainly the European ones and the Japanese yen. Accordingly the annual meeting of the IMF in Vienna in September 1961, was devoted to negotiations to set up an arrangement whereby the Fund could borrow the currencies it needed as quickly as possible. The so-called Group of Ten industrial nations (Belgium, Canada, France, West Germany, Italy, Japan, Holland, Sweden, Britain and the US) concluded an agreement ('The General Arrangement to Borrow'—sometimes known as GAB), whereby the IMF would be offered facilities to borrow up to $6,000 million on certain conditions. This helped to buttress the existing facilities provided by the IMF.

Since then further defences have been constructed, some of them specifically designed for particular currencies, such as the facility of $2,000 million (£833m.) set up in September 1968 to help the pound. This was part of a revolutionary arrangement designed to help sterling readjust its reserve currency role in the new circumstances following devaluation. It was (and is) known as the 'Basle Facility' and includes a standby credit put up by the governments and central banks of the United States, Germany, Holland, Belgium, Switzerland, Italy, France,

E   65

Austria, Sweden, Canada and Japan, on which Britain can draw over a three-year period whenever there is a fluctuation in the sterling balances held by the sterling area countries. A parallel agreement commits the overseas sterling area countries to keep a minimum proportion of their reserves in sterling, in return for an exchange guarantee from the United Kingdom.

The 'Basle Facility' was really the final part of a series of plans designed to relieve sterling of something of the double burden of being the currency of a deficit country, and a reserve currency of long standing. As we have explained its reserve currency role meant that large amounts of sterling were in the hands of foreign governments and individuals, mostly in the sterling area. As the governments of the sterling area countries grew alarmed about the future exchange stability of the pound, or as individuals did an increasing amount of their trade with countries other than Britain, there was a long-term tendency to 'diversify' : this is to hold currencies other than the pound, thus exchanging these holdings of pounds for Deutschmarks, dollars, or yen. A first attempt was made to deal with this particular sterling problem in September 1965, when new and specially flexible arrangements were set up with a group of central banks, including the BIS, and separately with France, totalling $1,000 million. These credits were renewed in June 1966 and again in following years to provide continuing facilities to cushion the impact on the reserves of any cashing-in of sterling balances held by governments and private individuals. At the time of the setting up of the Basle Facility it was decided that these earlier credits would be progressively liquidated and terminated by 1971.

Under the Basle Facility, drawings on the credit can be made up till 1971. There is no indication of what happens after that. But the White Paper in which the British Government announced the facility left the door open for one proposition which has been widely discussed. This is that a part of sterling's reserve function might be taken over by what are known as Special Drawing Rights, a new kind of world money. 'Although there has been much academic discussion of schemes by which some of the functions of sterling might be taken over by some new

66

international asset', said the White Paper ('The Basle Facility and the Sterling Area', Cmnd. 3787), 'no practical possibilities of this kind exist for the time being.' That was in 1968. But it has already been overtaken by events. The Special Drawing Rights scheme, which was originally worked out and approved in principle at the annual meeting of the International Monetary Fund in Rio de Janeiro in 1967, is now in operation and quantities of new world money (sometimes called 'paper-gold') have been distributed and will be held by central banks, alongside gold, pounds and dollars.

Special Drawing Rights or SDRs, therefore, are likely to provide, in the long run, the most lasting and constructive form of help within the international monetary system. Unlike reciprocal swaps and other post-war help, they are not designed as a stop-gap help for an individual currency in difficulties. They are intended to provide a lasting addition to the world's supply of international money. Apart from gold this at present is supplied almost entirely by the two reserve currencies, the pound and the dollar. As both the US and Britain succeed in their efforts to end their balance of payments deficits (Britain has already done so), this source will dry up.

The implications of the SDR Scheme are discussed in Chapter 15; its technicalities are described in more detail in Chapter 18. It will do little, in itself, to end the massive flows of speculative capital which have made the international monetary system so unstable in recent years. But by increasing the overall level of international reserves, it should give countries in difficulties a little more elbow-room to solve their problems, whether by financing a balance of payments deficit until domestic measures have time to work, or just by fending off a speculative attack with a larger pile of reserves.

It has sometimes been argued in recent years that the increasing sophistication of the means by which the international monetary community can help a country in difficulties has meant delays in the introduction of unpleasant measures to remove the cause of the difficulties. Certainly in the case of the British devaluation in November 1967, this argument has carried some conviction. The British Government might well

67

have been forced to devalue much earlier had it not been provided with the resources of other central banks to ward off speculators against sterling. Whether the delay was a good or a bad thing is still hotly debated by the economists.

Chapter 7

WHY IS GOLD USED?

*There can be no other criterion, no other standard than
gold. Yes, gold which never changes, which can be shaped
into ingots, bars, coins, which has no nationality and which
is eternally and universally accepted as the unalterable
fiduciary value par excellence.*
—General de Gaulle, February 1965.

*We need a quantum of international currency, which is
neither determined in an unpredictable and irrelevant
manner as, for example, by the technical progress of the
gold industry, nor subject to large variations depending on
the gold reserve policies of individual countries; but is
governed by the actual current requirements of world
commerce, and is also capable of deliberate expansion and
contraction to offset deflationary and inflationary tendencies
in effective world demand.*
—Lord Keynes, 1943.

We have so far devoted several chapters to the problem of
national currencies. It is time to turn to what many regard as the
most fascinating question of all: the role of gold. Why is it
used? Why do some countries wish to make it the lynch-pin of
international finance? And why do others, just as vehemently,
wish to banish its use for ever?

Man's fascination for gold is as old as civilization itself. Ever
since the yellow metal was first scraped out of the ground its
appeal to humanity has been universal. The great tombs of
Egypt, the Minoan civilization of Crete, ancient Rome—all had
succumbed to the charms of gold. Much of this lasting love is
based on good, practical reasons. Gold is virtually indestructible.
Unlike other metals it does not tarnish except under harsh
acid treatment. It has stood the test of time as shown by the
recovery of treasure from sunken ships and excavations by

69

archaeologists. Aesthetically, the appeal of gold is based on its flexibility and the ease with which craftsmen through the ages have been able to handle this most malleable of metals.

Its appeal is heightened by its universal acceptance. Whether one's arguments are based on reason or emotion, it is puerile to deny that gold has become accepted—in some parts of the world much more so than in others—as a symbol of financial security. Currencies come and go, lose their value or stay relatively strong. None of these doubts and fears has ever affected gold even though its price has been pegged for thirty-six years. In other words, gold has many of the qualities we set out earlier as essential for international money. Although gold has played an important role in international trade for centuries, although it formed the basis of many local currencies for generations, it is perhaps surprising that it did not become a major economic factor until the latter part of the last century. The reason is simply that there had been little gold about. Much of what there was about was hammered into trinkets or worked into elaborate jewelry. But there was never very much of it until the Russian discoveries in the Urals in the middle of the eighteenth century and the great gold rushes about a century later. California, Australia and finally the discovery of the huge deposits in South Africa transformed the role of gold in the affairs of men by bringing it right to the centre of economic life. Now it no longer was a question of gold coin or jewelry stored in the palaces of Eastern princes but of gold bars and ingots sitting in the vaults of the central banks of the great countries determining their 'wealth'. International debts were to be settled in gold and a country's trading position was to be measured by the amount of gold it held. And one cause for the seemingly insatiable demand for gold is that it has persistently been in short supply; that never at any time has the supply been able to match a steadily expanding demand.

Even today when gold production is still increasing in South Africa, which accounts for about three-quarters of the free world's supplies (there are no official figures on Russian gold output), not enough new gold is being produced to meet both official and private demand.

Moreover, the global quantities are still tiny in relation to any other leading 'commodity'. For example, today's gold stocks are put at something around 78,000 tons (worth around $85,000 million). Of this total, about 38,000 tons represent the Western world's gold monetary reserves. The balance, or some 40,000 tons, must be assumed to be in private hands—in jewelry, coins, hoards and speculative positions as well as gold in industrial use. The distribution of the world's gold, however, has changed dramatically with private stocks accounting for an ever-growing proportion. Between 1931 and 1947 private holdings remained steady at around 23,000 tons whereas new production almost doubled official stocks to around 33,000 tons. Since World War II the reverse has been the case: whereas monetary stocks have gone up by a mere 5,000 tons, gold in private hands has risen by 17,000 tons to 40,000 tons.

It is no coincidence that the private hoarding of gold has been concentrated in areas of traditional political and financial instability. Broadly speaking, the gold fetish is far more pronounced on the continent of Europe, especially France, in the Middle and Far East than, say, in Britain and the United States. And it was the French Government's decision in 1965 suddenly to exchange a large part of its official dollar holdings into gold which was to prove a watershed in post-war monetary history. For it was the first serious challenge to the present international system known as the gold exchange standard under which certain key currencies, notably dollars and sterling, are used alongside gold in national reserves.

Just how the gold exchange standard had worked and how it was augmented by the so-called 'two-tier' gold market system in 1968 we shall explain in greater detail in later chapters. Let us first remind ourselves of the uses of international money discussed earlier to explain the world monetary system. To work efficiently, international money must be widely acceptable; must be convenient to carrry and store; must be of consistent quality and if possible also indestructible; and should have some intrinsic value.

Gold clearly meets all these requirements and several of them more so than the leading currencies. For storing wealth both in

71

the official reserves of countries and private hoards it is highly suitable. Gold is valuable in relation to its size and weight; is of consistent quality and virtually indestructible. In addition, it has an aesthetic appeal. The combination of these factors had made it a desirable store or show of wealth in days long gone by when only small quantities were available. Gradually, as more and more gold was mined it became increasingly used, first as national money in the form of gold coins like Britain's sovereign, and later as international money.

With the growth of industrial society and the increase in money circulation it was found that paper money would be a more suitable unit of exchange—lighter to carry and easier to handle and acceptable as long as people had faith in it. And this faith was largely linked to the backing of the currency by precious metals and, since its universal acceptance, largely of gold. So, as gold became less important as a national currency, it became more important as an international payments unit. And its universal acceptance made it particularly suitable as a store of value in the central reserve of countries. Because of its intrinsic value there was little point in storing it as coin; much simpler, it was found, to keep it in bullion, or unminted form. It was because of this process of growing availability and nuiversal acceptance that countries have tended to hold at least part of their official store of wealth in gold.

Gold is also a convenient means of settling international debts. There is no longer any need to ship it physically from country to country. A visit to the gold vaults of any central banking institution is proof of that. The Federal Reserve Bank of New York is probably the finest example. Here hundreds of the 400-oz. bars—the standard unit used in central banking transactions—are heaped upon each other; usually in special compartments marked 'France', 'West Germany', 'Italy' and so on. When a settlement takes place it merely means a transfer from one compartment to another. Only France in recent years has insisted on having the gold she owns actually shipped to her rather than credited to her.

Private gold hoarding or storing dates back much farther. We have already touched on the awareness of the attraction of gold among earlier Mediterranean and Eastern civilizations; its lasting appeal for jewelry and other outward signs of wealth. When gold coinage was the order of the day last century, individuals tended to keep their savings for a rainy day in that form. More recently, there has been a tendency, especially in the Far East, Middle East and some continental countries to hold gold bullion (as well as gold coins) as part, if not all, of their savings.

In brief, gold's universal acceptance and intrinsic value has made it an ideal means of payment. First in coinage between merchants and traders; more recently to help settle the trading accounts between one country and another through respective central banks. Not all private citizens, however, are allowed to hold gold. Britain and the United States are notable examples of countries whose governments have banned private gold holding. But there is ample evidence that when inflation is at work and national currencies are suspect the attachment to gold tends to increase. For example, after the sterling devaluation in the autumn of 1967, British demand for gold coins, jewelry or gold 'sculpture' rose strongly.

There had been earlier evidence, too: the gold medallion wave of the early 1960s, for example, caught the British citizen's imagination. Here was a chance to hold gold almost in pure form, usually embossed with a famous historical figure for which the buyer paid a modest premium over the intrinsic gold value. So popular did these mintings become that the Chancellor of the Exchequer banned their issue in April 1966. Modern sculpture— frequently just any old lump—was another way of encouraging the gold fetish. As gold can be purchased for 'industry and the arts', here was another way around the gold holding ban and again the authorities stepped in to ban what they considered as a misuse of the trade freedom to buy gold.

If the British and American citizen has been less gold conscious in the past than his continental or Far Eastern counterpart, then this is thanks largely to the stability of his government and the relatively honest management of the national economy. Certainly, the most gold-minded of the Western countries, France, whose private gold holdings are estimated at

$6,000 million, or almost as much as the French official holdings at the peak of General de Gaulle's gold power in 1967,[1] has had more than its share of currency devaluations, internal inflation and political upheaval.

Probably because the holdings of gold, be it in a numbered account in a Swiss bank or under a farmer's bed in the Dordogne, has not been part of the Anglo-American way of life, and is of itself totally unproductive, the Anglo-Saxons are inclined to describe any form of private gold holding somewhat disparagingly as 'hoarding'. Maybe it is. But then it is scarcely any different from the tycoon who puts his money into valuable paintings or furniture and frequently keeps both in safe keeping, let alone the British or US citizen who buys gold jewelry for his wife—and not necessarily for adornment.

Gold is in every sense a barometer of international stability. As soon as there is a crisis, threat of a local war or, sometimes, even mere unrest inside a particular country, the demand for gold among the private 'hoarders' tends to go up sharply. In recent years, the recurring Middle East crises, the students' revolt in France in the summer of 1968; even the extreme right-wing party's gains in some German elections have all resulted in increased demand for gold. Broadly, there are two kinds of gold hoarders, European and Eastern. The European usually buys his gold through the traditional channels. Walking along Zürich's famed Bahnhofstrasse, every bank, big or small, will display a collection of gold coin or small pieces of bullion for sale. Anyone can step inside and buy a sovereign across the counter with no more formality than in a sweet-shop. Similarly, one can buy gold quite freely in West Germany and gold coins in France. The really large private holdings are naturally held on account of their owners by the big banks and are largely concentrated in Switzerland. Much international hot money or 'funk money', smuggled out to escape local taxes or put by for a rainy day by an acquisitive dictator or insecure monarch, is held in Switzerland in this way. Without entering the realm of James Bond, it is also true that many of the more dubious

[1] Peak figure for official French gold holdings was in November 1967 at $6,182m.

international payments (or should it be pay-offs ?) are made in gold.

In France, on the other hand, large quantities of gold are held in small amounts spread over a wide section of the population. The French farming community, in particular, has a tradition for holding part of its savings in gold. Much of this gold is held in private domestic hide-outs rather than at the banks because the owners tend to distrust the banks as much as the authorities. In Europe, then, by and large, gold is held by the rich or those with at least some savings who either distrust currencies or who wish to hold at least some gold among their holdings of stocks and shares, eurobonds, works of art or whatever.

For the investor anxious to acquire gold there is a fairly wide choice. Bullion, or gold in its raw pure form, is available in many sizes. Few private investors can either afford or would wish to be lumbered with the standard 400-oz. bar used by the central banks in their transactions. For the private holder there is the kilo bar worth something around $1,130, which is small enough to fit into a normal pocket, and several sizes downwards the 10-tola bar especially favoured in the East. This is worth some $132 and is a popular savings medium in India. Much smaller sizes of gold bars are produced too by metal refiners in Britain, France and Switzerland ranging from 5 grams to 100 grams and appeal more to the souvenir hunters than the gold hoarders. Speculators can also open a 'gold account' with banks in London and Zurich in which they simply hold the equivalent of a given number of ounces.

Gold coins are also a popular form of hoarding and hefty premiums are paid over the intrinsic gold value depending on the age and rarity of the coin. Local gold coins find favour with the residents of the country of origin. For example, the French are drawn to the 20-franc Napoleon d'Or, the Italians to a 20-lira piece and the Germans to a 20-mark gold coin. The US $20 Double Eagle is also popular. Ironically, the British gold sovereign probably enjoys the widest international distribution, even if British citizens are debarred from holding them. Gold sovereigns are still minted in Britain for distribution overseas and provide the Treasury with foreign currency revenue.

Whereas gold hoarding or gold buying in Europe is a

75

relatively simple and straightforward business, the real mystique of gold has its roots in the East. In the West gold customarily supplements other forms of savings media for those who are fortunate enough to have spare funds. Not so in the East where gold is a way of life, frequently even for those living at subsistence level. Just because India's millions are addicted to gold, the Government takes all precautions to suppress the gold inflow, though by no means completely successfully. The 'Golden Route to India', which Timothy Green describes in *The World of Gold*[1] must surely be the most romantic gold smuggling route of our day. It begins in the tiny sheikhdom of Dubai, one of the Trucial States at the southern tip of the Persian Gulf and about the third largest buyer of gold on the London market. From there the boats fan out across the Arabian sea to Karachi in West Pakistan and Bombay in India. This particular gold route provides the Sheikhdom of Dubai with high revenues and provides handsome profits for the intermediaries. The gold is flown to Dubai by leading London bullion dealers, including Samuel Montagu, and by the Swiss Bank Corporation. As it can be bought in Dubai at around the official level and is being sold in India at nearly twice the price— about $70 an ounce—the profit incentive is considerable even allowing for black market exchange rates. Dubai is by no means the only centre for gold shunting. Nearer Europe, Beirut has an active gold market and acts as centre for the Middle East, while Macao and Hong Kong are active centres looking after the gold requirements of the Far East.

A fair proportion of newly mined gold thus finds its way into the hoarder's hands each year. But the quantities so absorbed— be they $100 million or $200 million a year—are still not sufficient to explain the fact that year by year more newly mined gold is side-tracked into 'private' accounts and therefore provides no accretion to the official gold stocks which help to lubricate world trade.

We have tried to illustrate how the universal acceptance of gold has helped to give it a pre-eminent place in the world money system. We have also shown that a high proportion of

[1] *The World of Gold* by Timothy Green, published by Michael Joseph Ltd.

newly mined gold goes straight into private hands and that there is not sufficient new gold coming into the world reserves to cope with the expansion of world trade. Increasingly, therefore, the two key currencies, dollars and pounds, have been used to augment or supplement gold in official reserves; and hence they have become known as reserve currencies.

We have already described the evolution of these two currencies to reserve status; their growing use as trading currencies meant that more and more traders and bankers and eventually the central banks as well were content to hold part of their reserves in dollars and pounds. Especially, we have discussed earlier that as the share of gold in the world's reserves has been declining, so the use of the dollar has been growing persistently.

It follows then, that one difficulty surrounding the role of gold in the world monetary system is its availability. This raises the question whether it is either logical or desirable that world monetary affairs should be governed by the rate of mining of a particular metal in relatively few countries. Another difficulty is its price-level. The price of gold was fixed at $35 an ounce in 1934. It has stayed permanently at this level ever since. No other commodity has held its price-level over that period. It is not surprising, therefore, that both these problems—availability and price rigidity—have led to arguments about the use and future role of gold.

Sharp divisions in attitude persist among leading bankers and economists. There are those, like M. Jacques Rueff, the former French central banker, who see the only salvation in a return to a full gold standard—a system by which gold alone is used in international payments. He and his supporters have been urging a rise in the price of gold as the appropriate way of extracting more gold from private hands and of increasing world reserves and thus liquidity.

To M. Rueff the gold exchange standard, under which national currencies are used alongside gold in national reserves, 'is the product of a prodigious collective error which will remain in history and will eventually be recognised as an object of astonishment and scandal'.

On the other hand, there are those like Professor Robert

77

Triffin of Yale University (and Lord Keynes before him) who find the attachment to gold nothing short of absurd. 'Nobody could ever have conceived of a more absurd waste of human resources than to dig gold in distant corners of the earth for the sole purpose of transporting it and reburying it immediately in other deep holes, especially excavated to receive it and heavily guarded to protect it.' This is the school that is anxious to dethrone gold.

There is a third, middle of the road, school which believes in the *status quo*; this has also been the official American line which believes that the present price of gold should be held. Mr William McChesney, former chairman of the US Federal Reserve System in a speech barely a month before the March 1968 gold crisis said, 'I am firmly of the belief that a higher gold price is neither necessary nor desirable . . . I want to make it unmistakably clear that the future evolution of the system can and should be based on the present price of gold.'

Emotions clearly run high on the subject of gold. And these emotions have been fanned and the debate intensified with each successive currency crisis. For the lack of confidence manifested by the turbulence of the foreign exchange markets has tended to increase sharply the demand for gold. The first notable gold rush reflecting lack of confidence occurred in the autumn of 1960. This led to the setting up of the international gold pool. There followed minor eruptions but by and large the system held until the major crisis of March 1968 which led to the creation of what is known as the 'two-tier' gold market structure. We shall explain in detail the workings of these various systems in later chapters as well as the working of the gold market itself, but it is worth noting here the result of the two major changes. The lynch-pin of the gold exchange standard devised at Bretton Woods in 1944 was that the US Government was pledged to buy or sell gold to anyone at the price of $35 an ounce. This price set a yardstick for the price of gold on the 'free' markets, making allowance for the cost of transport and insurance. In theory, therefore, if the price on the free market rose substantially above that level, official supplies would be made available at the lower official price to meet the extra demand and bring the price back

78

again. In practice, this system worked until the autumn of 1960. On October 25th of that year, the price of gold on the London market jumped to $40.50 an ounce.

A variety of factors contributed to this particular gold crisis. Uncertainty about the US presidential election; the gaping US payments deficit, events in the Congo and the Middle East all conspired to spark off a sudden private demand for gold. The established machinery was unable to cope and the price shot up. The result of that day's activities was the creation of the International Gold Pool among the central banks of Belgium, Italy, the Netherlands, Switzerland, Germany, the UK and the US. All the members contributed gold quotas to the pool which acted (the Bank of England acting as its agent) as a stabilizing force to keep demand and supply in equilibrium and the price around the official level. The pool by buying and selling at the appropriate time managed to hold the situation until March 1968, when its supplies became depleted, the free London gold market was closed down and a conference hurriedly convened in Washington agreed on the 'two-tier' system. The two tiers were the official and private sectors of the system. Under this arrangement the leading central banks agreed to stay out of the private market altogether so that the private or free market became entirely dependent on the gold already in private hands. The gold producers, and especially South Africa, by far the biggest, were restrained from selling to anyone but the central banks.

To what extent the two-tier system has been successful still remains to be seen and will be discussed in a later chapter. Certainly, its introduction initially added to the uncertainties pervading world currency markets. Moreover, to those pundits who have been looking for a higher price of gold it has given fresh ammunition. They can now argue with some force that the gold exchange standard has been seriously undermined; that the attempt to hold the price of gold to the $35 an ounce parity has effectively been discontinued as has the convertibility of the major currencies into gold. With equal force, the anti-gold lobbyists have claimed a victory in that they see in the two-tier system a recognition that gold is no longer capable of playing its pre-eminent role in the world reserve system; that it has to be

79

supplemented by another reserve unit. Indeed, they can claim that the move towards activating the newly created 'paper-gold' reserve unit, the Special Drawing Rights (SDRs) from the IMF, was given a major boost as a result of the March 1968 gold rush.

To sum up then, gold has been universally accepted as a symbol of wealth and unit of exchange and, as a commodity, has played a major role in the affairs of man for centuries. It established its pre-eminence in world monetary affairs last century following the great gold discoveries in the US and South Africa. In recent years, rapid expansion of world trade has required more finance and there have been growing doubts as to whether sufficient gold will be available to lubricate world trade. One reason for the relative shortage has been the flow of gold into private hands, itself a reflection of political and economic uncertainties. World opinion on the future role of gold remains sharply divided but the view that some other international reserve units are needed to supplement gold has been gathering momentum and was given a fresh impetus following the March 1968 crisis and the establishment of the two-tier market.

Before we turn to the future role of gold, we need to take a look at the gold market itself.

Chapter 8

THE GOLD MARKETS

Nach Golde drängt, am Golde hängt doch alles.
—Goethe's *Faust.*

We have been concerned so far with the general use of gold and whether man will ever be able fully to control its contribution to the monetary system. The international debate on all this goes on. Yet every day a price is put on the value of gold in the London market. In spite of the interruption in new gold supplies from South Africa, London still sets the price guidelines for the world's free market. The whole financial world waits anxiously every weekday morning at 10.30 a.m. for the first intimation of the day's 'fixing' price. This City ritual takes place in a first-floor room of merchant bankers N. M. Rothschild & Sons in New Court, St Swithin's Lane, beneath portraits of several former European monarchs which serve as a vivid reminder of Rothschild's financial power in European politics during the last century.

The daily price 'fixing' ceremony itself is a simple affair. Five bullion houses are represented. Rothschilds act as hosts because they are agents for the Bank of England, which in turn used to act as agent for South Africa's Reserve Bank. Beside the hosts, there are present representatives of Moccatta & Goldsmid; Johnson, Matthey; Samuel Montagu; and Sharps, Pixley. The senior member of the bullion quintet is Moccatta & Goldsmid whose firm dates back to 1684, or ten years before the foundation of the Bank of England. When the Bank was established Moccatta's, who are now a wholly owned subsidiary of Hambros Bank, were appointed official silver dealers to the Bank. Second in seniority is Sharps, Pixley, a product of a merger in 1957 of two houses which began life in 1740 and 1852 respectively. Sharps, Pixley are now part of merchant bankers Kleinwort Bensons. Samuel Montagu, the merchant bankers and bullion dealers, entered the field in 1853.

F

Each firm represented at the 'fixing' (since April 1968 there have been two sessions each day) arrives armed with buying and selling orders from banking or industrial clients at home or abroad. Each member is linked by telephone to the trading room of his own house where, in turn, the dealers are in touch with clients in other centres. The representative of Rothschild's takes the chair. He has done so ever since the market was set up in its present form in 1919. The Chairman announces a starting price at a level which he thinks might bring buyers and sellers together. After reporting the price to his office, each member declares whether he is a buyer or seller or has no interest. Little flags are used to stop the fixing process. If the small Union Jack is kept upright a client is changing his position, i.e. hold up proceedings; if it is laid sideways the fixing may proceed. If he is a seller, the member declares at once—if possible—the number of bars he offers. Buyers at this stage are not required to specify their demands.

If, for example, all members declare themselves as buyers the price is moved up either until there are sufficient sellers to satisfy the demand or until the potential buyers refuse to bid a higher price. If they refuse to bid any higher they have to be prepared to accept a pro-rata share of the amount of gold offered. If, on the other hand, sellers predominate, the price will be lowered in stages until the buyers' demands absorb the gold on offer. When buying and selling orders are finally married, then the price for the day is fixed.

After the fixing, the members of the market return to their respective offices and continue to deal. They will deal between themselves, with clients the world over or with other banks authorized to trade in gold but who are not members of the gold market. Once fixed, the forces of supply and demand come into real play and the price will fluctuate accordingly. The morning fixing is simply a guideline.

To maintain a fluid market there must be a two-way traffic—demand as well as supply. Until the market's freedom was restricted in March 1968, which we shall explain in a moment, the demand for gold came from three main quarters: speculators or hoarders, the central banks and industry. We have already tried to show in the previous chapter that there is a traditional leaning towards gold as a savings and hoarding medium in certain parts of the world. We shall also discuss the speculative movements which have contributed to some of the more recent currency and gold crises in the next chapter. Certainly, it remains extremely difficult to put figures on the actual private demand for gold. Much of the flow goes unrecorded. What we do know is that private stocks have been accounting for an ever-growing proportion of total gold holdings. Industrial demand for gold has also been on a rising curve. Far and away the main industrial use of gold is in jewelry. Other consumers include the electronics industry, dentistry and decorative trades.

Samuel Montagu estimated in their recent *Annual Bullion Review* that industrial demand now approaches 60 per cent of production in the Western world. Much of this demand used to be met by supplies from individual countries' central banks—until March 1968 a major force in the gold market.

In the first instance, the buyers of gold are mostly the banks. They, in turn, will re-sell the gold either to other banks who may be acting for private clients or on their own account or even for some of the smaller central banks; the gold may be intended for fabrication into jewelry and will thus go to industry. Much of the gold bought through London will go towards supplying other gold markets which we will describe later in this chapter.

No market, however, can flourish without a steady source of supply. And one reason why London became the leading gold-dealing centre when the free market was reopened in 1954 was its traditional link with the leading producer countries of the Commonwealth, notably South Africa. Of an estimated world gold production in 1969 (excluding Russia) of 40·6 million fine ounces, South Africa produced over 31 million ounces, or nearly 77 per cent of the total. Canadian, Australian and West African gold also traditionally finds its way to London. Not least, the Soviet Union found London the most convenient centre for large-scale gold sales to help her balance of payments. For some years Soviet gold sales were running at a high level—between 1958 and 1966 at around £90 million a year. Indeed, when the wheat crisis of 1963–64 forced Russia to buy large amounts of

83

Table II. *United Kingdom Imports and Exports of Gold Bullion**
(*amounts shown represent Troy Ounces Fine Gold Contents*)

IMPORTS	1969 REFINED In bar Good delivery in London	1969 UNREFINED Including refined Not good delivery in London	1968 REFINED In bars Good delivery in London	1968 UNREFINED Including refined Not good delivery in London	1967 REFINED In bars Good delivery in London	1967 UNREFINED Including refined Not good delivery in London
Australia	—	—	23,781	—	—	—
Belgium	2,877,561	81,108	35,131	23,858	5,593	6,409
France	363,071	322	231,572	7,361	369,703	41,361
Germany (East)	161,575	—	64,507	—	—	—
Germany (West)	119,486	54,013	34,019	11,434	9,659	1,952
Ghana	—	723,656	—	737,620	—	764,058
Japan	—	238	—	—	10,452	5,360
Kenya	—	18,222	—	32,845	—	30,404
Lebanon	—	—	1,600	6,667	—	420
Liberia	—	—	—	19,957	—	—
Netherlands	22,427	1,120	3,725	1,241	—	—
South Africa	5,457,559	—	8,945,546	—	32,892,069	—
Switzerland	3,627,066	3,264	537,005	23,445	—	—
Tanzania	1,161	15,681	—	19,968	1,312	26,019
United States of America	—	—	34,341,424	6,750	—	—
U.S.S.R.	—	—	321,584	—	385,199	—
Other Countries	99,242	14,957	2,102	2,529	1,494	4,592
Total	12,729,148	912,581	44,541,996	893,675	33,675,481	880,575

PORTS	1969 REFINED In bars Good delivery in London	1969 Other forms	1968 REFINED In bars Good delivery in London	1968 Other forms	1967 REFINED In bars Good delivery in London	1967 Other forms
gentina	—	—	—	6,457	—	14,260
ustralia	61,349	459	—	25	1,299,051	—
ustria	48,275	—	709,582	—	14,048	4,333,822
hrain, Kuwait, Qatar and Trucial States	—	2,069,117	—	3,969,278	288,401	492,996
lgium	40,017	172,226	319,033	368,777	—	5,841
azil	—	27,139	—	26,016	—	60,470
unei	—	27,660	—	29,450	26,894	252,815
nada	—	143	20,353	125,826	—	240
ile	42,642	—	17,504	—	—	—
ina	475,729	—	1,808,082	3	—	9,974
prus	—	7,350	—	8,554	22,712	17,024
echoslovakia	92,843	12,850	46,331	29,925	1,607	53,129
nmark	—	49,937	1,207	45,528	—	13,817
e	—	26,990	—	22,751	499,734	—
ance	514,268	1,884	11,970,837	42,735	12,134,863	153,949
rmany (East)	26,151	289	1,938,011	128	1,487,030	9,785
rmany (West)	247,393	72,475	1,415,309	152,418	3,059,779	154,181
eece	—	25,377	—	62,496	1,599	39,426
ng Kong	—	507,543	—	201,381	—	13,373
ngary	—	—	144,910	—	—	45
lonesia	—	1,929	—	6,527	—	14,165
n	161,799	6	193,390	51	—	—
ael	—	72,131	4,381	45,301	1,571	56,645
ly	124,337	5,405	2,008,073	1,589	1,416,969	6,478
pan	1,158,375	7,780	319,282	8,604	—	37,557
os	—	249,942	66,670	223,100	4,864	81,177
banon	—	830,727	184,564	1,296,055	507,494	1,909,486
oya	503,821	64,294	—	32,147	887,198	83,616
xembourg	—	—	9,410	19,963	10,464	11,895
acao	303,183	—	298,837	—	1,226,253	—
alaysia	—	153,273	—	40,679	—	30,450
alta	—	8,012	—	9,734	—	11,621
therlands	397,571	119,048	829,958	41,781	756,695	127,939
therlands Antilles	—	—	—	17,991	42,769	62,265
rway	21,970	5,626	30,566	5,786	30,574	9,691
land	—	25	31,897	—	—	—
idi Arabia, Iraq, Muscat and Oman	4,829	41,453	8,040	73,432	72,483	19,935
gapore	—	189,725	119,934	117,546	—	113,403
ain	80,404	2	193,695	—	135,440	—
eden	65,468	18,718	75,497	18,291	148,748	30,963
itzerland	1,333,191	319,429	22,454,261	1,663,032	26,680,494	1,400,150
ailand	4,805	193	32,396	18,420	—	2,950
rkey	—	4,095	—	8,258	—	2,950
ited States of America	215,553	166,698	657,636	280,410	11,640	41,048
her Countries	4,059	33,620	4,483	40,864	1,606	37,646
Total	5,928,032	5,293,570	45,914,129	9,061,309	50,770,980	9,714,227

* Source: *Samuel Montagu's Annual Bullion Review 1968* and *1969*.

Canadian wheat which had to be paid for in hard currency, the Soviet gold sales are estimated to have reached twice that figure in a single year. In more recent years, the Soviet Union has been a less active force on the gold market.

Just how much gold is being traded on the London market— or for that matter any other gold market—remains one of the mysteries surrounding the gold trade. Accurate statistics on trading figures are not available. The London gold market has never revealed its turnover but some measure of its activities can be gleaned from Britain's import and export figures (see Table II).

As a result of the distortions brought about by the disruption of supplies from South Africa following the March 1968 crisis, the 1967 figures give a more realistic picture of the traditional import pattern and show the flow of gold towards London from South Africa (until March 1968) and other Commonwealth areas. Again, the export figures highlight the huge demand for gold from Switzerland and France during 1967 and 1968. Italy and Germany (both East and West) also were large buyers of gold in the period covered by the table. The 1969 figures reflect the changes in the trading pattern following the establishment of the two-tier system: UK imports were a mere $13\frac{1}{2}$ million ounces against $45\frac{1}{2}$ million ounces the year before, whilst exports fell from 55 million ounces to $11\frac{1}{4}$ million ounces.

We have already indicated that the gold crisis of March 1968 which led to the setting up of the two-tier gold market structure was to be a major turning-point both for the future role of gold in world monetary affairs and the London gold market itself. To try to put this into perspective it is worth recalling what had made London the undisputed gold centre until then. After all, the London market had been closed from the outbreak of World War II in 1939 until 1954.

When it did reopen in 1954 it had to make up the ground lost in the intervening period to Zurich. It managed to do this for two main reasons. In the first place, London was able to attract the supplies and resume its traditional role for marketing South African gold. Secondly, the London banks eager to re-establish their position deliberately cut their dealing margins to well below the Swiss banks' level and thus recaptured the market by direct competition. Much of the rising turnover in the first few years was due to central bank activity. It has been estimated that by 1956 the central banks were responsible for about one-third and a year later for about one-half of the total turnover in London.

When the pound became freely convertible in 1958, new opportunities for expanding the London gold market were quickly grasped. More bullion business followed in the wake of increased continental currency dealings. At the same time, convertibility brought with it new strains and stresses. Whilst European currencies became stronger, the dollar became increasingly suspect. We have already referred to the first notable gold rush in October 1960 brought about by a crisis of confidence. This saw the first official intervention. As the gold price broke through from around $35 to $40 an ounce strong official action was needed. The Bank of England, accustomed to act on its own account or on behalf of the South African Reserve Bank on this occasion moved into the market on behalf of the US authorities. Official selling managed to steady the market and bring the price down again. More significant, this move marked the beginning of central banking co-operation in controlling the gold market. The realization that leading central banks acting in concert could do much to stabilize the gold price led, a year later, to the creation of the International Gold Pool.

Under this arrangement, the central banks of Belgium, France, Italy, the Netherlands, Switzerland, West Germany and Britain agreed to co-operate with the US Federal Reserve Bank of New York. This sales consortium was to be run by the Bank of England who was able to draw on supplies of gold from member banks to intervene and steady the market. Quotas were agreed with the US providing half of the supplies.

The pool's fortunes fluctuated. First set up to deal with a sudden demand for gold which was threatening the official price level, the market soon turned the other way with the pool being able to purchase gold to support a falling market. In 1963 for instance the pool managed to share out among its members $600 million worth of gold. The pool's existence, however, also

87

had some important repercussions on the operations of the gold market. It meant that central bank buying on the free market almost dried up completely. Those central banks who were members of the pool tended to transact their business through the pool thereby depriving the gold market of an important slice of turnover.

For the next few years, however, the international bankers' pool was successful in stabilizing the price of gold and in dealing with any speculative pressures that arose—until its surrender in mid-March 1968. The first fortnight of March that year saw an unprecedented speculative demand for gold with the pool having to provide an estimated $3,000 million worth of gold. According to Samuel Montagu the central bankers' pool supplied the market between January 1st and March 14th with 45 million ounces —or just about equivalent to the entire Western world's output for a year.

On March 14th the pool abdicated and the following day the market was officially closed. The Governors of the seven banks constituting the pool rushed to Washington for a panic meeting. The result was a new arrangement, the closure of the London gold market for another fortnight, and the emergence of the 'two-tier system'. The policy was outlined in the official communiqué: 'The Governors believe that henceforth officially held gold should be used only to effect transfers among monetary authorities, and, therefore, they decided no longer to supply gold to the London gold market or any other gold market. Moreover, as the existing stock of monetary gold is sufficient in view of the prospective establishment of the facility for Special Drawing Rights, they no longer feel it is necessary to buy gold from the market. Finally, they agreed that henceforth they will not sell gold to monetary authorities to replace gold sold in private markets.'[1]

This gold crisis marked the end of an era. The London market was closed on official orders from March 15th until April 1st. When it did reopen it did so on the basis of two price fixings a day, at 10.30 a.m. and 3.00., the second fixing setting the guidelines for North American activity. Since then, too, the fixing price

[1] See also Chapter 15.

for gold has been expressed in US dollars per fine ounce instead of sterling. With the gold pool's former members now agreeing not to deal through the free market and with South Africa's sales policy still in balance, a good part of the London market's former activity dried up although as an international dealing centre it remains unsurpassed. At the same time, speculative activity has been enhanced by the uncertainties surrounding future reforms of the monetary system and anxieties on specific currencies.

If the central bank's demand has dried up, the commercial banks and Eastern dealers appear more active than ever. The latter buy the metal for resale to private hoarders, i.e. citizens who consider gold as the safest and best investment. These dealers, and certainly their customers, are normally willing to pay a premium over the 'official' or shipping parity price. This has been demonstrated since the March 1968 crisis when on occasions the price of gold on the free market crept up to over $43 an ounce: not to speak of the little private gold rush in Paris during the financial crisis of March 1969 when a gold kilo bar reached the equivalent of $48 an ounce.

For the London gold market, the enforced closure in the spring of 1968 was a bitter blow. It gave its major rival Zurich a tremendous opportunity to expand its own business. As the only major Western dealing centre during this turbulent fortnight and with so much speculative gold moved into Switzerland in the preceding months, the Swiss banks were better placed than ever to recapture some of London's business.

Zurich was undoubtedly in a strong position. The Swiss banks were, as always, holding huge quantities of gold for their international clients. Switzerland is in any event a gold-conscious country. A modest investment in gold is quite commonplace, though Swiss citizens have never been known as gold hoarders. They have had no reason to hoard, thanks to their innate and well-deserved trust in their own currency. And the enviable stability of the Swiss currency is in no small measure due to the fact that the country has traditionally attracted such a large volume of international funds including gold. Add to this the total financial freedom and it is scarcely surprising that an active gold market should have developed throughout the land though it is centred on Zurich.

This market undoubtedly gained a considerable fillip during and after the March 1968 crisis. If hitherto the Swiss banks—and the bulk of the gold is in the hands of the three giants (Swiss Bank Corporation, Union Bank of Switzerland and Swiss Credit Bank)—have been known to deal in big volumes among themselves, their international activities were boosted strongly by London's shut down. There is increasing evidence, too, of the Swiss banks' bullion activity in the Middle East and Far East, once considered very much the London market's territories.

The Swiss banks clearly enjoy certain advantages. They are well equipped to meet sudden flurries of demand because they always have large stocks of gold, mostly held on behalf of clients. This is in contrast to the London market which believes more in rapid turnover than in taking big positions, i.e. holding large stocks. Again, the Swiss banks have under local banking laws to keep 5 per cent of their deposits either in gold or on deposit with the Swiss central bank—at no interest. They prefer usually to keep this balance in gold. As a retail market in gold, Switerland is clearly extremely important; as a wholesaler London still has the edge.

Since the introduction of the two-tier system, the Swiss banks have also been actively courting South Africa in an attempt to obtain marketing rights for at least some of South Africa's new gold. Their success in this direction is likely to be a major determination in the future rivalry between Zurich and London. For the time being it is thought that the London bullion dealers' widespread network of agents throughout the world keeps them ahead in the international marketing of gold. But it would be rash to suggest that London has held its absolute dominance of the pre-1968 years.

If London and Zurich are today the world's most important gold markets, they are by no means the only ones. As far as Europe is concerned there are active internal markets both in Paris and Frankfurt. Paris has traditionally had a large domestic turnover because of the French citizen's huge appetite for gold already described. Frankfurt has developed its gold-dealing activities in step with growing West German prosperity and the German citizen's almost pathological fear of inflation. In the international context, however, one has to move towards the Middle and Far East, to Beirut, Hong Kong and Macao to flavour the twilight world of official and thoroughly unofficial dealings in gold. Beirut has for long been a distribution centre for the Middle East and many places far beyond. Gold shunting has become a local industry and the authorities seem quite content to see it go on. Beirut's position is strengthened by the fact that the Lebanese Government permits the free import and export of gold whilst many of its neighbours do not. Much of Beirut's gold supplies comes from London and a high proportion is in the form of kilo bars. Those bearing the stamp of London's Johnson, Matthey are particularly popular. In recent years, too, the market for gold coins has expanded with British sovereigns still much sought after. However, due to Middle Eastern attitudes to the sexes, the current series of sovereigns bearing the Queen's head are not favoured! Greater demand for gold coins has given a stimulus to the forging industry and excellent replicas of sovereigns or French Napoleons and American double eagles are now being produced locally.

In former days, too, Beirut served as the distribution centre for gold destined for India. Much of this gold now bypasses Beirut and goes direct from London to Dubai. Again, much of the gold that used to move via Beirut to the Far East is these days shipped direct to Bangkok, to Laos and, of course, to Hong Kong. Hong Kong and its twin centre, the Portuguese colony of Macao, are engaged in an intricate pattern of gold dealing. Syndicates are at work here which have discovered ways of satisfying the huge demand for (smuggled) gold all over South East Asia, India, Japan and some think even mainland China. The gold arrives officially enough at Hong Kong, usually by air freight from London. It is then removed to Macao where much of it is melted down into small ingots more convenient for smuggling back into Hong Kong for further distribution. On the way from Hong Kong to Macao the gold is carried quite openly, usually by hydrofoil across the 40 miles of the mouth of the Pearl River. On its way back it is carried by a variety of

passengers and transport—less openly. Once safely back in
Hong Kong the gold moves from the vaults of the six leading
dealers through the Chinese Gold and Silver Exchange to the
many Chinese banks and money change offices that abound in
Hong Kong. A good part of it bypasses the Exchange altogether, and goes direct from the dealers to major jewelry interests and the like. The reason for this extraordinary carry-on,
the shunting between Hong Kong and Macao, is simply this:
within the colony of Hong Kong gold may be held and exchanged freely. But the import and export of it are forbidden.
How long these particular manœuvres will continue will depend
on how long tiny Macao will be allowed to exist as a so-called
independent unit on the tip of China. Already the Portuguese
administration is scarcely more than a sham. For the time being
it clearly suits China to have this independent loophole. If it
were to go, the entire distribution pattern of the Far East would
have to be redrawn.

So much then for the leading gold-dealing centres of the
world. We have tried to show that gold markets flourish in
many parts of the globe; that man's trust and belief in gold has
so far remained uhshaken although it varies greatly among
different peoples and areas. As far as the Western world is
concerned, London and Zurich are by far the most important
gold markets. Their activities are determined by the state of
public confidence in currencies and hence in domestic or international economic policies. A sudden demand for gold can be
sparked off by equally sudden speculative onslaughts; the leading central banks have evolved a number of different arrangements culminating in March 1968 with the dissolution of the
gold pool and the setting up of the two-tier market. Since then
the debate on the role of gold in world monetary affairs has
continued; since then, too, 'paper-gold' or the IMF's Special
Drawing Rights have actually been activated.[1] But meantime,
too, there are dealers all over the world hanging on the telephone
each weekday morning waiting for the gold market's key guidelines—the price of the day's fixing decided in a private banker's
room in the City of London.

[1] Referred to in Chapters 6 and 15; full details are given in Chapter 18.

Chapter 9

WHO ARE THE GNOMES?

*I think that we should perhaps eliminate from our thoughts
the somewhat naïve caricature that what has been going on
is a machination of some bearded troglodytes deep below
ground speculating in foreign currencies for private gain.*
—Mr Harold Wilson, July 27, 1968.

The telephone lines from the private bankers' room at the daily
gold fixing in New Court, described in the last chapter, may well
lead direct to the 'speculators' and 'gnomes' in all parts of the
world. Who are these speculators, these sinister 'gnomes' or
even 'troglodytes' who seem to be set on undermining the world's
monetary system? In this chapter we shall try to disentangle
speculation from commercial prudence and to explain just what
causes the rushes into particular currencies and out of others.
    Whether we are talking about the gnomes of Zurich or the
'dunderheads of Basle' (Mr Michael Foot's copyright, we believe), the principle is much the same. The blame for what has
gone wrong with the pound (or any other currency for that
matter) is being quietly placed elsewhere. This attitude was
naturally at its height during the alarming run on the pound in
the autumn and winter of 1964 when the new Labour Government came face to face with its first sterling crisis. Mr Henry
Brandon has since described the attitude of the Labour
ministers in the following terms:

'The Ministers began to see again the old familiar spectre of an
international conspiracy against Labour; the conspiracy in the
phrase coined by George Brown, of the "Gnomes of Zurich".
And whenever he used it, and he did not use it sparingly, he
rolled the "g" and the "n" separately off his tongue with an
expression of disgust and disclaim on his face. The "Gnomes of
Zurich" became a winged phrase and Mr Wilson and Mr

Callaghan adopted it almost as soon as Mr Brown had launched it.' [1]

In fact the phrase 'the Gnomes of Zurich' has a much longer ancestry. Mr Peter Thorneycroft was calling them just that in the autumn of 1957 when still Chancellor of the Exchequer. 'I must be hard-faced enough', he declared during an earlier sterling crisis, 'to match the mirror-image of an imaginary hard-faced little man in Zurich.' And later the same year Mr Andrew Shonfield, then Economic Editor of the *Observer*, was sadly reflecting in his book, *British Economic Policy Since the War*, how tough it was on the Swiss that William Tell should have been displaced in English folklore 'by this new image of a gnome in a bank at the end of a telephone line'.

Now the legend has gained reality. It is no longer unknown for a Swiss banker to appear on British television, describe himself as a typical gnome of Zurich and explain what the other gnomes are thinking about Britain and the pound. Even if they did not exist, Britain would have invented them. Indeed many people are firmly convinced that that is the truth about the whole affair.

Yet if they do exist and admit to their existence, what exactly do they do, and how can they be recognized? This, alas, is where much of the confusion begins. They are said to have two main characteristics. In the first place gnomes are regarded as devious foreign financiers speculating against the pound for private gain. Secondly, they are also regarded as giving Britain financial help but only in return for following their own hard-faced policies. As Michael Foot once put it succinctly 'They'll never be really satisfied until they see us pulling down our hospitals and schools with our own bare hands'. This double-image is one of the main misconceptions. The first, if true, is simply a description of a private banker operating for his own ends. The second, again if true, is an equally simple description of a central banker (the Swiss National Bank, the Bank of France, the German Bundesbank) giving official help to the Bank of England on some of his

[1] Henry Brandon: *In the Red. The Struggle for Sterling* 1964–6, Andre Deutsch, 1966.

own terms. Far too often in the public mind (and clearly the minds of left-wing politicians) the two are merged into a single identity. The fact of the matter is that the first will get Britain into trouble; the second will help to bale her out. The first is a real gnome; the second simply a part of the official network of international monetary co-operation we have already described.

Why are gnomes apparently born and bred in Zurich? Is it just a peculiar characteristic of the Swiss or of that part of Switzerland? Perhaps Swiss bankers do have a flair for international monetary affairs lacking in, say, Paris, Amsterdam or Brussels. But in our view, the difference is more technical than human. Switzerland became the focal point of international finance after the war for special reasons. It had not suffered the ravages of war. It was not burdened with the need for reconstruction. It was not troubled with financial debts. It had escaped the wartime and immediate post-war inflationary pressures, still active elsewhere.

Prosperity, therefore, was widespread in Switzerland. Prices were stable and there was confidence in the Swiss franc. On top of which the Swiss market was active and the banking network intact. It was natural that if London bankers still had too much to occupy them at home, Zurich bankers would step into their shoes. So they did—for a while. Basically Zurich provided a freedom of movement not available or possible elsewhere. Gold could be bought and sold freely and so could other foreign currencies. Banking secrecy helped: numbered accounts, with no questions asked, were the final touch in Zurich's favour. This combination eventually led to the quick establishment of a market in transferable sterling, a form of sterling provided to the bulk of Britain's foreign customers. They could use it anywhere in the transferable sterling area, which was already the non-dollar part of the world. At the same time sterling acquired by people in the dollar area had a different 'tag' attached to it. The market provided by Zurich bankers simply ensured that holders of these different sorts of sterling could switch into gold and other currencies—at a price. And the price was the so-called free rate for sterling in Zurich, often quoted at a significant discount on the official dollar–sterling rate.

If the rate dropped sharply, the gnomes were thought to be at work. It was a convenient shorthand for speculation as well as for normal commercial transactions. It was also a convenient label for politicians keen to offload some of the blame for sterling's weakness elsewhere. In short, for special technical reasons, Zurich had made the market and correspondingly took the blame, even when the people buying and (particularly) selling sterling could be of any other nationality. When the convertibility of the pound, on December 29, 1958, switched most of these currency dealings back to London (along with the bulk of the Zurich gold business) Zurich lost a large slice of its business, but not its gnome-like reputation. Though it no longer dominated currency deals, it was still a convenient shorthand for what was in future likely to be going on just as much in Paris, Amsterdam, Milan, Frankfurt, Brussels, or indeed London, as in Zurich.

All this explains why gnomes originated and are still thought to exist in Zurich. It does not explain what they do, or why they do it. Britain is troubled with gnomes for a simple reason. As we explained, sterling is a major international trading currency; it is also one of the two main world reserve currencies. In short, both traders and governments want to hold it. They find it convenient to do so. But, occasionally, if foreign holders of pounds begin to suspect that Britain's economic policy is too inflationary or they lose faith in the Government's ability to ward off inflationary pressures, they may feel that they are running too great a risk in continuing to hold pounds. They decide to take their sterling balances from London, until their confidence has been restored. When they do this on a large enough scale, it leads to their own central banks being offered large amounts of sterling in exchange for their own currency. And when this sterling is offered to the Bank of England, in exchange for gold or other currencies, the result is a rapid fall in Britain's gold reserves. A run on the pound has started and the gnomes, it is said, are at it again.

Now the gnomes, as we have already explained, are basically commercial bankers operating either own their on behalf or, more likely, on behalf of clients. Far from being gnomes they are veritable giants in the financial sense because they control

96

a good part of that international money pool which is frequently described as hot money. The pool itself is made up of a large number of segments. There are the balances of the great international rich; the funds held on behalf of the oil sheikhs of the Middle East; there are the thousands of smaller secret accounts which tot up to a formidable total; and there are the balances of the great international trading companies whose worldwide operations require access to funds in many parts of the world at short notice. What the Swiss bankers think and do therefore does matter and since it is their duty to look after their clients in the best possible way it is also their duty to find the most profitable outlets for their funds. Sometimes this may mean buying gold on hopes of a rise in the price of gold; at others it will involve shifting balances into Deutschmarks on hopes of revaluation or out of sterling on fears of devaluation. The bankers can, of course, be so convinced that sterling is overvalued that they think that they might make money out of an eventual devaluation. They might, therefore, try to speculate against the pound in whichever way they can. But this is not as easy as it is often made out to be. Selling something you do not already possess has its difficulties, even in the world of currencies. Greater banking responsibility and fairly tight controls in a number of countries have seen to that. Any respectable bank today would require some evidence that a foreign exchange operation of a non-banking client is for genuine commercial purposes. There is, in any case, enough trouble in coping with people who already have pounds or assets in Britain or even potential earnings from Britain to get over-anxious about outright speculation. It is usually action arising from the possession of sterling, sterling assets or sterling earnings by foreigners that causes most of the trouble put down to the gnomes. That foreign commercial bankers undertake these actions on behalf of foreign residents and that Zurich bankers are efficient in international transactions is usually sufficient evidence for most people that the Zurich gnomes are 'speculating against the pound'. That they are simply protecting their clients' interests is too often ignored. Yet this is the main motive behind most recent runs on the pound.

G   97

It can, also, of course, be initiated by people living in Britain. Gnomes are not unknown in London, or in the streets of Manchester. If a British firm has the need to pay in foreign currency immediately ahead and becomes convinced that, by delaying such a payment, it may be running the risk of having to pay 15 or 20 per cent more in the event of a sterling devaluation, it may feel that it has every reason to pay promptly. And it instructs its bank accordingly. Potential holidaymakers can do the same by drawing out French francs, Italian lire, Swiss francs, etc., from their banks weeks or even months before they are actually going on holiday. There is, of course, a limit to some of these actions since the holding of foreign currency can run counter to the exchange control regulations.

The main point to understand, however, is that fears for any currency will persuade many people either to delay payments or to hurry them along. If the pound is under suspicion British residents are likely to be persuaded to pay up sooner for their imports and to acquire foreign currency for spending abroad sooner. On the other hand foreign residents will be persuaded to delay the receipt of sterling in the hope that the exchange rate may have changed in their favour by the time that the payment is effected. All these are the so-called 'leads and lags' in payments that give sterling so much trouble during a currency crisis—briefly referred to in Chapter 5.

We have, therefore, distinguished three different types of currency manipulations: (a) outright speculation; (b) switching of funds out of sterling; and (c) changes in the timing of payments.

All three can be, and are, put down to the gnomes. They are, of course, mainly blamed for the first—speculation. Yet contrary to most assumptions, the biggest pressures on the pound come from the second and third categories; and there is little doubt that the third is potentially the biggest and the most dangerous of all. Consider why. Britain is a major trading nation. In a year Britain's imports amount to some £6,000 million. Exports add up to over £5,000 million. All these payments can be increased or delayed according to the anxieties or worries of the traders involved. Nor is this all. The whole of the sterling area uses sterling in its trade both with Britain and the rest of the world. It has thus been calculated that if payment for all sterling area imports from the rest of the world for just one week were made one week earlier this could cost Britain's gold reserves £150 million immediately. If legitimate traders can, because of their anxieties about the pound, put such pressure on the gold reserves by the simple process of changing the timing of their payments, it is hardly necessary to look under too many beds in Zurich or to root out the gnomes in trying to establish the culprits.

Yet whether gnomes are simply hard-faced speculators or good Continental bankers advising their clients how to protect their legitimate trading interests, their influence on British economic policy has still to be considered. This is where the original distinction between commercial bankers and central bankers becomes important. The former can have no direct influence on policy. Indirectly, of course, a knowledge of their views and activities can provide a rough guide to how they would react to different policies: and this in turn may show whether the Government's incomes policy, for example, will reassure them or simply lead to a removal of surplus funds from London. If confidence in the currency is strong, the gnomes will hardly concern themselves with social policy or government spending in general. But if confidence is less robust, policy towards the unions, for example, can be an item that may swing sentiment and lead to an outflow of funds from London. To this extent even commercial gnomes can be said to influence policy. Yet it is only the weakness of the pound that puts such pressure in their hands and the weakness of the pound must result from economic mistakes perpetrated either in Whitehall or in the economy generally.

The influence of the central bankers is quite another matter. As we have already outlined, these are basically the members of the so-called 'Basle Club'—the leading European and North American central banks that meet monthly at the Bank for International Settlements in Basle. They are the bankers who provided Britain with short-term credit and credit facilities: the Bank of France, the Federal Reserve Bank of New York, the

German Bundesbank, the Bank of Italy, etc. And such help is unlikely to be forthcoming without Britain being given a pretty good idea what policies would find favour among her creditors and what would not. Written agreements are not necessary in this fraternity and are rarely asked for. But most borrowers are given to understand what is expected of them. These are not the gnomes. To some extent they attempt to offset the work of the gnomes. But they too come in for their share of the kicks.

HOW IT HAS WORKED

Chapter 10

THE DAYS OF THE GOLD STANDARD

We are striving to return to the normal, which ultimately means a gold standard. . . . This policy has worked well. It has generally been accepted by the public here and by those abroad, and, if followed out, will go as far as anything to reinstate the finances of this country.
—Mr Montagu Norman, Governor of the Bank of England, in his first speech as Governor at the Bankers' Dinner, Mansion House, July 15, 1920.

So far we have been trying to explain how the world's monetary mechanism works and why it works the way it does. This has already led us down several interesting byways both before and since the war. But these excursions were undertaken with particular purposes in mind, as illustrations of our analysis as we went along. It is time, therefore, with the equipment already provided, to take a longer journey over recent monetary history. In the next four chapters we shall look at the way the world's money system has been developing, from the gold standard (in this chapter) to the new 'paper gold'.

It may have been a yearning for the golden days of Pax Britannica. It may have been an intellectual longing for the simplicity of the *laissez-faire* economics of the last century. Or it may just have been that the magic of the metal twisted men's perception. But for many years after its demise in 1914 the nineteenth-century gold standard was held up by most economists and politicians as some sort of economic land of milk and honey. In popular mythology it still retains that place today. But the myth of the gold standard is like many other myths. It only grew up after the situation it purported to describe had passed away. Yet it also contained a grain of truth. Our task in this chapter will be to separate fact from fiction.

We need to start with the gold standard as it was popularly supposed to have worked, a belief encouraged to a large extent by the Cunliffe Report of 1918. This was the first official effort to describe and explain how the international payments system had operated in the period since the Report of the Bullion Committee of 1810. During the years when the system was running smoothly, no one worried very much why. Only after it had disappeared, did all the self-searching analysis begin.

Before we set out how the gold standard was believed to have worked, we need to explain, briefly, the differences between various systems, some of which we have already mentioned in earlier chapters. A country is said to be on the gold standard when its currency can be switched into gold at a fixed price. Thus when sovereigns were circulating in Britain before 1914, the country was on the full gold standard. Later, when sovereigns had disappeared but the Bank of England was still willing to buy and sell gold at fixed prices, Britain was said to be on a gold bullion standard. In both cases there was a link between the gold reserves of the country concerned and its domestic currency.

The pure gold standard was said to have worked roughly as follows: In international payments, most transactions were financed by buying and selling commercial bills denominated in foreign currencies or sterling. But ultimately any debts between countries which were not cancelled out by credits were settled in gold. International movements of gold then had a related impact on the national currency and, through it, on the domestic economy. The amount of a national currency in circulation was closely tied to the amount of gold in a country's national reserves. In Britain after 1844 almost all of the note issue of the Bank of England had to be covered, pound for pound, by gold or silver. In many other countries, the size of the note issue was determined by a minimum proportionate reserve ratio.

According to theory, these links between the amount of gold in the vaults of the central banks and the amount of domestic currency in circulation meant that when a country was in deficit, gold would flow out of the reserves to settle its payments, and the volume of the domestic currency (coins and notes in

104

circulation) would be correspondingly reduced. This would tighten the supply of money and reduce the availability of credit, lowering the domestic demand for goods and causing a fall in prices. Imports would fall with domestic demand, and exports would rise as goods became cheaper, and, hey presto, the trade balance would move from deficit to surplus. All this was fairly automatic.

There were, however, one or two controls that could be used. The Bank of England could assist the whole process by altering Bank Rate, that is, the prime rate of interest that in turn affects most other rates of interest. It could also manipulate credit by buying or selling government securities. If gold was flowing out of the country, the Bank would raise Bank Rate and restrict credit; if gold was coming in it would lower Bank Rate and expand credit. This had two effects (so the theory ran): in the first place it would speed up the decline in business activity by increasing the cost of credit as well as its availability, and secondly, in the short run it would enable the Bank to stem the outflow of gold by making it more profitable to hold gold in London.

This, at any rate, was the Cunliffe Committee's description of the system. And the Report summed up the whole mechanism in this revealing passage:

'There was, therefore, an automatic machinery by which the volume of purchasing power in this country was continuously adjusted to world prices of commodities in general. Domestic prices were automatically regulated so as to prevent excessive imports; and the creation of banking credit was so controlled that banking could be safely permitted a freedom from State interference which would not have been possible under a less rigid currency system.'

This was a comforting account of a system that seemed to be so badly needed in the rudderless world of 1918. But, unfortunately, this analysis, even allowing for its simplified form, is inadequate and misleading. It is now generally agreed that it is far too simple a picture of the way in which the gold standard

105

actually worked. We have set it out in this way for a particular reason. This simplified, semi-automatic system was the carrot that led so many people to press for its re-introduction as soon as possible after 1918. And the differences between this hopeful vision and the harsh reality were wide enough to foster the misconceptions and disasters of the late 1920s and early 1930s.

There were four major differences. In the first place the theoretical framework contained some important flaws. Secondly, the system was kept going more by the dominant role of Britain and sterling in world trade than anything else. Thirdly, the system was far more managed than many people realized. Fourthly, it had not solved the major problem of unemployment. We can look at these separately. Let us look at the theoretical weakness first. The theory does not allow for the effect that a decrease in economic activity will have on imports— it only looks at the effects of changes in the price level on the trade position. More seriously, it assumes that the general level of economic activity is highly sensitive to changes in the rate of interest. Current experience suggests that the cost of finance may not be quite so important, and that the main domestic effect of a change in Bank Rate is psychological. In addition, the assumption that exports and imports are sufficiently sensitive to price changes to affect the trade position is at best doubtful. Lastly, this version of the gold standard ignores the effect of Britain's policies on overseas countries.

Yet even if the popular version is faulty, the fact is that the system worked. There must, therefore, have been other features that somehow compensated for these inadequacies. It is now suggested that these involved the special position of Britain as the main trading and capital-exporting nation of the world, the pre-eminence of the City of London as the financial capital, and the leading role that sterling played in lubricating the system. We explained earlier how the 'bill on London' was used worldwide for the financing of trade both within and between countries. It also played a crucial part in the adjustment process, that is the way in which changes took place in the world economy. At any one time there was a large volume of short-term sterling credits moving about the world. It was this sterling, not gold, that an increase in Bank Rate attracted back to London. The increase in Bank Rate pushed up the discount rate (that is the rate of interest) on commercial bills of exchange[1] as well as on government bills. As a result it either became more profitable to discount (that is sell) the short-term sterling bills in London than in other centres or the increasing cost of borrowing in sterling meant that sterling facilities were used rather less than those of other currencies. In either case the amount of short-term sterling borrowed in London declined, thus easing the demands on the gold reserves. Some gold, of course, was also attracted by the higher Bank Rate, but it was only in severe periods of financial stringency (for example in the Baring Crisis of 1890 when Baring's, the august merchant bank, nearly went bankrupt) that the amount reached large proportions.

Britain's position as a capital exporter helped the adjustment process in another way. A large part of her foreign lending was tied to purchases of British goods. Thus the level of her exports did not depend so much on their prices but on the flow of foreign lending. As a result a rise in the export of British capital was usually accompanied by a boom in exports and vice versa. Thus we have two major reasons why the adjustment process managed to take place without too much strain. The first (the link between exports and capital exports) was more substantial. But both were tied inextricably to Britain's special position.

Moreover, it is now realized that the gold standard was much more 'managed' than the Cunliffe Committee was prepared to believe. The connection between flows of gold and the level of domestic credit, even in Britain, was not quite as close or as automatic, as the gold standard theory made out. The fact is that the Bank of England could and did vary the reserve in its 'Banking Department'. This could be used to 'sterilize' movements of gold into and out of the country so that they did not alter the level of credit at home. It was by this means, for example, that the Bank was able to mitigate the effect of gold discoveries in Australia, the United States and Canada (and the gold famines in between) in the second half of the nineteenth

[1] These are promises to pay a certain amount on a certain date.

century. To this extent even Britain, despite her advantages, had to 'manage' the system.

As for other countries, many were not as closely linked to the gold standard as seems to be assumed. Thus in the early years of this century, apart from Britain, only the United States and Holland in practice permitted the export of gold without restriction (and this was when the system was thought to be in its most classic form). Before 1870 most European countries were on a bi-metallic standard using both gold and silver. The US formally adopted gold as the sole backing for the dollar as late as 1893. Other countries in fact were on what has rather charmingly been called a 'limping' gold standard, where notes could only be changed into legal tender, silver coins (and not gold), if the authorities so decided. Even when countries were on a full gold standard they often adopted technical methods for discouraging the export of gold. Indeed the Bank of England offered advances free of interest to finance gold imports during the Boer War.

Finally, although Britain was able to build up her industry and trade and her overseas investment (in short her wealth and power as a nation) because of the workings of the gold standard, the system's main flaw must not be forgotten; this was its inability to control the ups and downs of the trade cycle. Throughout the nineteenth century there were alternating booms and slumps in economic activity and in price-levels. Worse, unemployment would rise to perhaps 10 per cent at a time of slump, before falling back to 2 per cent in a boom. These rapid and uncontrolled changes worried, even alarmed, economists and social historians. But the hardship caused was generally thought to be an inescapable cost of industrial society. This acceptance of unemployment, coupled with the misconceptions of how the gold standard had worked, was to lead to several errors in economic policy in the 1920s.

To sum up, the gold standard's success was based more on the dominance of Britain in world trade than on any other factors; and it was less automatic and less all-embracing than generally assumed. It had not solved the problem of unemployment. Its re-introduction in 1925 ignored the decline in Britain's world position, the change in sterling's status and, above all, the dangers in re-imposing the system with the wrong sterling exchange rate.

Chapter 11

1929

No Congress of the United States ever assembled, on surveying the state of the Union, has met with a more pleasing prospect than that which appears at the present time. In the domestic field there is tranquillity and contentment . . . and the highest record of prosperity. In the foreign field there is peace, the goodwill which comes from mutual understanding. . . .
—President Coolidge, December 4, 1928.

Twice this century leading governments of the world have tried to set up a system for international payments that would ensure the unimpeded growth of world trade. The second attempt—in 1944—is still working itself out and we shall be considering it in a later chapter. But the first effort in the mid-1920s failed miserably, stability lasting no more than four or five years. It is instructive to see why.

From the start of the 1914–18 war virtually all gold payments were suspended and all enemy assets were generally seized. Sterling exchange rates (and those of all other Allied currencies) fluctuated widely, but later this was prevented by official action, pegging the rate. When these rates were freed in 1919 there followed a period of fluctuations and speculation. The exchange rates of the victorious countries tended to slip downwards; those of the defeated slumped. Faced with this confusion, the one aim of most governments was to get back to the orderliness of the gold standard, as quickly as possible.

But as we saw in the last chapter, the current idea of how the gold standard had worked was faulty in two respects: it was not appreciated how far the smooth functioning of the gold standard was dependent on the special position of Britain and of sterling; it was also not realized the extent to which the system had been 'managed'. It was thought that by recreating the institution of gold, the system would run itself.

110

This determination to restore gold was reinforced by the collapse of the German mark in 1921–23. Other currencies also declined: particularly those of Austria, Hungary and Poland. But it was the fate of the mark that caught the imagination. Burdened by reparation payments and with a shattered economy on its hands, the German administration resorted to printing money to pay its debts. The effect was immediate and disastrous. By 1923 it took a 50-million-mark piece (about the size of a ginger nut biscuit) to buy a loaf of bread. Many of the middle classes were ruined, the savings of a lifetime wiped out. When the mark was finally stabilized it was at a rate of one million million times that of 1914.

Britain's determination to return to the gold standard was reinforced by these post-war problems and as soon as Britain's war debts and German reparations were on their way to a solution the Bank of England turned to the conditions and the timing of such a move. After much discussion (mainly about the exchange rate rather than the restoration), Mr Winston Churchill, as Chancellor of the Exchequer, announced the return to gold on April 28, 1925. Gold exports were again permitted and the Bank of England announced that it would buy gold at £3 17s 6d an ounce and sell it at £3 17s 10½d—its pre-war parity. The main difference between this new version and the pre-war gold standard was that the metal was no longer in domestic circulation—pound notes could no longer be converted directly into gold. So if anyone wanted to export gold, it had to be done in the form of bullion at a minimum cost of several thousand pounds. Apart from this, however, the main features of the pre-war mechanism were resurrected.

The Commonwealth followed Britain's lead, also returning to gold in 1925, and were joined by the Netherlands and Hungary. Soon most European countries were back on the gold standard, with the French franc stabilized in 1926, and the Italian lira a year later.

Then, from 1927 to 1931 a brief period of exchange stability emerged. But those four years were an uneasy calm, with parities only maintained at the cost of considerable strain. The central problem was the relationship between sterling and the

French franc, with the overvaluation of the pound and the undervaluation of the franc measured against dollars. The reason for the misalignments were purely political. The pound was fixed at its pre-war parity so that it 'could look the dollar in the face'. The franc, for its part, was fixed at a low level to give France a competitive advantage in international trade, which indeed it did.

These problems were recognized at the time. When the pound returned to the gold standard in 1925 it was thought to be about 5 per cent out of line (though it was probably nearer 10 per cent too high in relation to the dollar). But because of the faith the British politicians had in the gold standard mechanism, this difficulty was confidently expected to disappear as British wages and prices fell. As we now recognize, it is extremely difficult to push wages and prices downwards and they are certainly less flexible than the crude gold standard theory led people to expect. It took a General Strike in 1926—sparked off by the attempt to drive down miners' wages—to prove the point.

Internationally the imbalance between the pound and the franc caused a rush of gold to Paris. According to the gold standard theory, as we explained in the last chapter, this ought to have caused a rise in French price-levels to cure the imbalance. This did not happen in the main because the French authorities did not 'play the game'. Instead of allowing the inflow of gold to lead to an increase in the domestic money supply, it was 'sterilized', that is the automatic link between France's gold reserves and her domestic currency was severed.

In fact stability in the foreign exchange markets was only maintained by keeping London interest rates higher than those in other financial centres. This attracted hot money (that is, mobile short-term funds) at the expense of aggravating domestic depression. Worse, this hot money was liable to disappear as quickly as it had arrived. All it needed was a serious economic crisis to bring down the whole edifice. That came in 1929 with the collapse of Wall Street.

The spectre of the 1930s continues to haunt all who lived through them. But for the purpose of this book we need not concern ourselves with the complex interrelation of cause and effect that lead to that catastrophe. We shall have a few things to say on the economic forces at work in a later chapter. What does concern us at present is the currency manipulations of politicians as they tried to preserve what they could of their countries' prosperity and the effect this had on the state of mind of the men of 1944—their resolve to avoid the mistakes of the 1930s.

During this decade most countries had attempted to boost their declining exports by depreciating their currency. As we explained earlier, in theory the 'cheaper' a currency is in relation to others the easier traders should find it to export. As every country found its exports declining, it tried to depress the price of its own currency.

It did not take long for the effects of the Wall Street slump of 1929 to be translated into economic decline and currency crisis. Volume after volume has been devoted to the analysis of why it all happened and we shall be considering some of the main factors later. For our present purpose let us set out, briefly and simply, the main features leading to the collapse of sterling in 1931.

(*a*) Fall in wholesale prices (they were down 25 per cent between 1929 and 1931). Rising unemployment (up from 10 per cent in October 1929 to 18½ per cent in October 1930 and to 22 per cent a year later).

(*b*) UK balance of payments problem—the current account— was £103 million in credit in 1929, and then swung round to a £104 million deficit in 1931.

(*c*) Falling tax yields—the budget went into deficit and impaired confidence in the pound.

(*d*) Flight of funds from Germany in June 1931—German banks got into serious trouble causing other financial institutions in Europe to look at their own liquidity and want gold.

(*e*) £32 million of gold withdrawn from London in second fortnight of July. Bank Rate pushed up and Bank of England negotiated credits with Bank of France and Federal Reserve Bank of New York (end July). Political crisis in UK—Labour Government resigned in late August.

H   113

(f) Although new National Government negotiated new loans, withdrawal of funds continued in early September.

(g) On September 15 news of 'unrest' in Royal Navy.

(h) On September 18 it became clear that new credits on necessary scale would not be available.

(i) September 19 (a Saturday) decision made to suspend gold standard, and announced the next day (September 20th).

(j) Monday, September 21st, a Bill amending the 1925 Act restoring the gold standard was rushed through Parliament and Bank Rate raised to 6 per cent.

The pound was then allowed to 'float' and find its own level against other currencies and so was permitted to depreciate in terms of gold. A number of other currencies tied themselves to sterling (most of the Commonwealth plus a few others) to become the sterling area. Most countries tried to remain on the gold standard for as long as possible. Yet one by one they fell. After sterling the next to go was the dollar, which collapsed in April 1933 after a series of spectacular banking failures. The reasons for the suspension of the gold standard in the US were different from those in Britain. In the UK external pressures were uppermost. In the US, the gold standard was regarded as a stumbling-block to any efforts to increase domestic prices so desperately needed by American farmers. But the American suspension had international repercussions. At the World Economic Conference of July 1933 President Roosevelt refused to consider stabilizing the dollar in case it would harm US export opportunities, and later that year he made specific the policy of not giving the dollar a fixed price in terms of gold. In fact, of course, the dollar was stabilized in January 1934, but at a level (against gold) 60 per cent lower than before. Such a massive devaluation quickly transferred pressure to those countries that still maintained the link with gold—the so-called 'gold bloc'—and in particular to the French franc. For a while, despite the burden on the gold bloc of overvalued currencies, this situation continued. But in 1935 came the first collapse. Belgium devalued by 28 per cent, putting the Belgian franc roughly in line with sterling. Italy, involved in the Abyssinian

War, left the bloc later that year. The French franc maintained its value until 1936, but then it was repeatedly devalued until a rate was finally found at which it would be held in the autumn of 1938.

Sometimes currencies were pegged for a while at a certain level. But often during this period they were allowed to fluctuate as they wanted to. To add to this confusion governments backed up competitive devaluations with restrictive trade and exchange policies. Germany, for example, managed to maintain her exports by a system of various types of marks, quoted at different rates for different countries and even for different types of goods. In Latin America the situation was even more complicated as, in addition to this type of practice, exporters were allowed to keep part of their foreign exchange earnings and resell them on the free market at a considerable premium.

The net result of this confusion was that not only did world trade collapse; the prerequisites for its revival were not present.

The relationships between the various things that went wrong are complex. But it is worth trying to sort out the main features.

1. *The initial parity imbalance*
In 1925, when sterling returned to the gold standard the pound was—for prestige reasons—overvalued against the dollar by around 10 per cent. The French franc was undervalued by about the same amount.

2. *Failure to adjust*
(*a*) Britain—the overvaluation was realized, but it was thought that it would be possible to get British costs, including wages, down by the necessary amount. The General Strike of 1926 proved this idea wrong.

(*b*) France—the undervaluation resulted in an inflow of gold. But instead of allowing this to increase the credit base, and so push up French costs, this gold was 'sterilized' and hoarded.

3. *The dependence on short-term money*
In order to maintain the position of sterling Britain was forced to rely on hot money inflows. This money was attracted by

holding interest rates in London above those in New York. This worked against the economic needs of both the UK and the US. Britain needed low interest rates to stimulate production; the US high ones to help curb the Wall Street boom. Worse, the hot money on which Britain was depending was to depart rapidly in 1931 forcing sterling to leave the gold standard.

4. *The rise of protectionism*
Countries, including Britain, resorted to import controls and tariffs to try to reduce imports and so stimulate home production.

5. *Export Promotion*
The other method by which countries tried to stimulate home production was by increasing exports (a mutually defeating process when set against (4) above). This was done in two main ways: by currency manipulation (i.e. competitive devaluations and multiple exchange rates) and by export subsidies.

6. *Currency blocs*
The rise of protectionism led to the creation of currency blocs (for example, the sterling area).

7. *Currency fluctuations*
The system of floating rates adopted by many countries (after they were forced off gold) made international trade increasingly difficult.

8. *Fall in reserve assets*
The fact that currencies like sterling were no longer acceptable to the same extent in international trade reduced the volume of assets available. Thus countries were forced to depend even more on gold.

Such was the tale of woe. It led to a decline in international trade, which in turn led to a decline in world production and economic activity, rising unemployment and all the hardships of the greatest depression the world has ever known.

It was against this background that the post-war monetary

system of fixed exchange rates and the IMF was born. Any system of international exchanges must do two things: it must provide enough liquidity, that is international money, for countries running payments deficits to have a breathing space to get into equilibrium, without having to introduce restrictive trade policies; and it must provide for the adjustment of exchange parities when things have got too far out of line for a natural recovery to be possible. As we have just seen, the gold bullion standard as operated from 1925 to 1939 did neither.

Chapter 12

THE BIRTH OF CURRENCY BLOCS

Even during the period when Rome lost much of her
ancient prestige, an Indian traveller observed that trade all
over the world was operated with the aid of Roman gold
coins which were accepted and admired everywhere.
—Paul Einzig, *Primitive Money*, 1949.

Before we continue our historical narrative and consider what
has been happening since the Second World War, we now
need to pause for a moment to look more closely at one of the
phenomena of the 1930s, the rise of currency blocs.

Ever since Alexander the Great, most conquering powers
have tried to impose their own currency on the territories they
control. Alexander, for example, brought a common monetary
system, based on Athenian coins, to all the lands he conquered.
Such a policy often has strong political reasons—apart from
the gratification a ruler gets from seeing his portrait passed
from hand to hand throughout his dominions.[1] These reasons
usually centre round the early realization that a common
currency is a powerful weapon in binding disparate lands
together. A common currency is administratively convenient
and can encourage inter-regional trade. It can also be used to
cut off the economies of the countries within the empire from
the outside world. From the policies of Alexander the Great
to those of Brezhnev and Kosygin is a small step.

Yet not all currency blocs are so restrictive. Often they arise
more out of convenience than imposition. This has happened,
as we saw in Chapter 4 and in the last chapter, in the case of
the group of countries joined together by sterling. In addition

[1] Alexander was unlucky. His head did not appear on coins until after his
death; not until later was the idea of using the head of a *reigning* monarch on
coins introduced by the Syrians.

118

to the sterling area there are two other main blocs today, the French franc zone and the Iron Curtain countries, linked in Comecon,[1] as well as the remaining traces of the dollar area, formed round the United States, in the inter-war period. These four blocs are obviously very different in form. As we have seen, the sterling area is a loose association of countries all over the globe, some of which used to be part of the Empire, some of which just found it useful to be members. The French franc zone, on the other hand, consists in the main of former French territories and is much more tightly knit. In contrast to both of these the dollar area numbers countries like Canada which have little more than historical ties with the US dollar. As for the Comecon countries they are clearly in quite a different situation, being subject to political as well as economic pressures and being outside the West's monetary system.

These blocs, however, have a number of things in common. They all have relative freedom of currency movements internally plus some form of common currency barrier between them and the outside world. Both trade and capital tend to flow between countries within the region rather than to countries outside it, while one currency—that of the major country in the bloc—is usually preferred as a vehicle for these payments. On the other hand they have been formed in two quite separate ways. One group (Alexander the Great and Comecon) by imposition, the other group (the sterling and French franc areas) by mutual convenience. The first, as one might imagine, leads to a rigid authoritarian body; the second to a looser group linked merely by mutual interest. But sometimes the second type is cemented by outside pressures into a tight defensive unit. This is what happened with the sterling area.

The Sterling Area

For the start of the sterling area we have to go back to the beginning of the eighteenth century. A Royal Proclamation of Queen Anne in 1704, backed by an Act of Parliament three years later, established a standard based on the Spanish silver dollar (the 'piece of eight' of *Treasure Island* fame) to link

[1] Comecon: The Council for Mutual Economic Aid.

colonial currencies in North America and the West Indies. What in fact happened was that, with the collapse of the Spanish Empire, sterling tended to become the standard of value rather than the Spanish coin. There was no move to impose the British currency as a medium of exchange (as opposed to a standard of value) until more than a hundred years after. Then in 1825 a Treasury minute proposed that 'the best standard of circulation for the British colonies and possessions . . . will be the silver and copper currencies now in circulation in this country, provided the same be made convertible, at the will of the holder, into the standard gold currency of the United Kingdom. . . .'

As it happened, it took more than legislation to establish sterling throughout the Empire. The rupee (then based on silver, not gold) remained the currency of India and in the West Indies a number of individual currencies continue to be in use today. Bahamian dollars, for example, are connected to sterling not the US dollar. But some parts of the Empire, notably Canada, allied themselves with the United States dollar rather than the pound. Despite these anomalies the commercial power of Britain and the pre-eminence of the pound sterling for trading purposes made it convenient for most of the Empire to link its currencies closely to sterling. It was thus common interest, not legislation, that established sterling's international role. It was regulations that sustained it, however, for the whole character of the area was changed during the 1930s.

When sterling left the gold standard in 1931 the countries of the sterling area were faced with a choice: to go along with the pound or to maintain a separate link with gold. Most, though not all, chose to throw in their lot with sterling, thus forming the basis of the sterling area as we know it today. There were many reasons behind their choice. Since part of their reserves were in sterling, had they maintained their link with gold there would have been heavy paper losses on their reserves. More important, much of their trade was with Britain and the Dominions and a stable relationship with these trading partners was more attractive than one with other countries who remained in the so-called gold bloc. Even more fundamentally, in those chaotic days sterling perhaps looked a more stable partner than some other currencies. Thus not only the former Empire countries, but also countries like Egypt, Argentina and Japan all made the decision to join what then came to be known as the 'sterling bloc'.

This association was reinforced by several special factors. The Ottawa tariff agreement of 1932 establishing Imperial Preference (a system where Commonwealth countries gave imports from other members preferential tariff treatment),[1] and also a bilateral trade agreement with Scandinavian and Baltic countries boosted trade within the area at the expense of outside countries. Moreover the relatively early recovery of the UK from the depression helped to stimulate demand for imports from countries in the area. The bloc was cemented by economic necessity, with the countries within it following similar monetary and trade policies in an effort to pull themselves out of the depression by their bootstraps. This operation met with some degree of success: the recovery of prices and trade within the area before the rest of the world was quickly recognized. Other blocs emerged, most notably that built round the dollar, while the French colonies followed the franc. In 1936 these developments were institutionalized by the tripartite monetary agreement between sterling, the dollar and the franc.

Immediately before the war, therefore, the picture was of two main blocs, sterling and the dollar, with a much smaller cluster round the franc. But at that stage the edges of both the two big areas remained vague. Some countries, like Argentina and Japan, moved in and out of the blocs as convenient; others, like Canada, remained in a sort of half-way house in between them. However, from the onset of the war the sterling area ceased to be an informal body: it became a single administrative unit.

On September 3, 1939, Britain introduced a set of exchange controls which effectively cut off sterling from other currencies, though transactions within the sterling area—this title was formally introduced the following June—remained free of these

[1] I.e. the import duty on goods from Commonwealth countries was lower than that on goods from other countries.

121

controls. To start with, the area consisted of the Commonwealth minus Canada, Newfoundland and Hong Kong—countries which would almost automatically support British currency policy. Later other countries were added: Egypt, the Sudan, Iraq; and eventually the Belgian Congo, plus various 'free French' colonies.

We have already explained (in Chapter 4) how the sterling area maintained its cohesion both during and immediately after the war—largely through economic circumstances. Yet in recent years there has been a considerable loosening of the ties that bind the area together. In the first place, the return to convertibility for holders of sterling outside the UK removed the main distinction between sterling and the dollar. Convertibility simply meant that pounds could be switched into dollars quite freely. Thus the levelling out of the balance of economic power between the dollar countries and the rest of the world—the ending of the so-called dollar shortage—also ended the need to discriminate against that currency.

Secondly and connected with this, the removal of world trade barriers under GATT[1] has reflected a general broadening of trade relationships. Commonwealth preference arrangements have been losing their force. For one thing, trade in manufactured goods has risen far faster than trade in commodities. Accordingly Britain no longer wants to trade solely or mainly with the Commonwealth, and vice versa. From Britain's point of view, the most attractive and fastest-growing markets have been other industrialized states. The growth of her exports to the Common Market and her decision to join the European Free Trade Association have both reflected this shift in emphasis. As a result sterling area countries, for their part, have attempted to reduce their dependence on one market by selling to other industrialized countries.

Thirdly, Britain is no longer able to supply most of the capital needs of Commonwealth countries. Her recurrent balance of payments deficit has led her to limit overseas lending to the sterling area (using the weapon of 'moral suasion'

[1] Gatt, the General Agreement on Tariffs and Trade, is the post-war organization devoted to the removal of tariff barriers.

so as to avoid the odium that more direct methods would attract) as well as to the outside world. Other industrial countries, in particular the US, have been quick to fill the gap, while the volume of international lending through the World Bank has also tended to replace sterling loans. Moreover the UK payments deficit (plus the two post-war devaluations) has also undermined confidence in sterling as a reserve currency. Lastly the granting of political independence to virtually all the Commonwealth has removed the automatic link between local currencies and sterling, quite apart from any effects it may have had on trade policies of the emergent countries.

The weakening of ties is manifesting itself in several ways. Already we can point to two specific examples. The first is that the proportion of sterling held in the reserves of sterling area countries is steadily declining, with the preference for both gold and dollars increasing. The second example is that several sterling area countries did not devalue with sterling in 1967, in contrast to 1949 when not only the sterling area but many other parts of the world followed the pound. This was in marked contrast to the 1969 devaluation of the franc, when virtually all the French franc countries immediately followed suit.

The Franc Area

The differences between these two recent devaluations—of the franc and of the pound—are a good pointer to the differences between the two areas. The franc area, or at least the inner part of it, maintains a close relationship with Paris. This part consists of the former French African colonies linked in the CFA franc (this originally stood for Colonies Français d'Afrique, but was later changed to Communaute Financière Africaine). The fourteen members of this group, countries like Senegal, Chad and Mali, were not even consulted before the last French franc devaluation, even though the institutional arrangements forced them to follow suit. The CFA franc is guaranteed by the French Treasury; the Bank of France holds the reserves of the area; there is complete freedom of movement between the two currencies; and France even has a measure of control over the credit policies of CFA franc countries. She also appoints

123

representatives to sit on the boards of the CFA issuing banks.

There is also, however, an outer franc area consisting of the three North African states, Morocco, Algeria and Tunisia, which is much more like the sterling area. Their currencies are defined in relation to gold, not in relation to the French franc. Though they do have a special relationship with France—in the form of preferential trade and financial agreements—they act independently on currency matters. In the summer of 1969 they proved this independence by refusing to follow the franc down.

This experience once again illustrates the features which bind together and separate blocs. In the case of the CFA, members still have the sort of agreement that used to hold the sterling area together. France supplies the capital needs of these countries (her foreign aid is almost entirely directed to former colonies) and is therefore able to exert a degree of political control that would be impossible for the UK. On the other hand, where aid payments are less important and the connection is based on trade relationships, as with the North African countries, the unity of the bloc tends to suffer.

The Comecon Countries
When we examine Comecon we are again talking of a body of countries cemented by political authority. Though the bloc ostensibly exists to promote trade between Eastern European countries and the Soviet Union, it is fair to say that it has often been used by Russia as a means of pursuing her own economic policies. Certainly as a means of increasing international trade it has not been particularly successful. The Comecon countries, with 31 per cent of the world's industrial output, only manage to generate 10 per cent of its trade. It is because of the way it is organized that it has not developed real freedom of trade within itself. Trade is still based on a series of bilateral agreements (that is agreements between two countries). This, plus the Communist system of pricing, makes the normal functions of international trade (outlined in Chapter 1) almost impossible.

The important thing to remember when looking at the East European countries and the Soviet Union is that the prices of

124

goods in the shops bear little relation to their cost of production. Prices are fixed by decree. This means that all the normal relationships between prices within a country no longer work. Thus the money used to buy wheat could be more valuable than that used to buy potatoes, or vice versa. When this system is extended to the international sphere the difficulties simply spread over a wider area. Consider the following description:

'When selling to the Soviet Union compressors for, say one million roubles, Czechoslovakia expects that this money will enable them to buy oil or aircraft at agreed prices. It would be very disappointing to find that all it could get were Bulgarian tomatoes at prices arranged on the assumption that these will be paid by textiles. If trade were a matter of money instead of the detailed commodity lists which are part of the bilateral trade pacts, this is what would happen and Czechoslovakia would discover that by paying with compressors for tomatoes, it spent possibly 20 times the labour required for building the greenhouses and cultivating tomatoes at home.'

This was written by an East European journalist[1] now in exile in the UK.

It is not hard to see the reasons why at least some of the Comecon countries want to preserve this system. It enables the USSR, for one, to force countries like Czechoslovakia to 'invest' in its industry with the surplus balances of roubles it accumulates on trade account. But the damage it is doing to the bulk of the Eastern bloc is now increasingly being recognized. There have been repeated efforts to institute multilateral payments (though the USSR is still anxious to preserve the advantages it gets from the present system). Out of the proposed moves one in particular has a familiar ring to Western ears: to form a 'convertible rouble' for international payments. For the idea is that this rouble should be linked to gold. Apparently even the might of international Communism cannot escape from Lord Keynes's 'barbarous relic'. The Soviet Union, having discovered the growing disadvantages of bilateral trade patterns,

[1] Adolf Hermann, *The Banker*, March 1969, pp. 239–40.

125

is now, like Alexander the Great, intent on imposing its will by the widespread use of its own currency, golden or otherwise. As George Orwell might have put it, the members of some currency blocs are more equal than others.

Chapter 13

BRETTON WOODS AND AFTER

*The international monetary system can never be a rigid
system, with fixed and permanent arrangements. It must
be such that it can develop with the varying growth of the
individual national economies, and with the evolution of
their financial and monetary needs and potentialities.*
—Per Jacobsson, Managing Director of IMF 1956–1963,
speaking in New York in April 1961.

After the break in the last chapter to explain how and why
currency blocs are created, we must now pick up the historical
threads again. We have already explained how the Bretton
Woods monetary system came into being and discussed the
ideals behind it. It was based on the lessons learnt from the
chaos of the 1930s: on the need for stable exchange rates; on
the need to oil the wheels of trade by ensuring an adequate
supply of reserves; and, although this came later on, the need
to provide development capital for poorer nations. It was to
provide these three factors that the three bodies of the Bretton
Woods Conference were proposed: the International Monetary
Fund, the International Trade Organization, and the International Bank for Reconstruction and Development (the World
Bank). In fact, only two of these bodies got under way. The
ITO was stillborn because of opposition from the US Congress,
the General Agreement on Tariffs and Trade (GATT) being
substituted in its place as a compromise solution. So we are
concerned with the way the IMF, the World Bank and the rest
of the Bretton Woods system managed to cope with the post-
war situation. It is to this question that we now turn.

The one fundamental problem that the whole system was to
run up against will quickly become clear. The arrangements
were created at a time when the US was at the height of its
power. Europe was shattered, Japan was in the process of

127

THE WORLD'S MONEY

being destroyed, and the dollar, backed by massive gold reserves, was supreme. The Conference reflected this situation. At that time the dollar was indeed as good as gold, and so it remained throughout the early post-war years. But as American supremacy was gradually eroded, especially from the late 1950s onwards, the strength of the Bretton Woods system was also undermined.

Before we give the impression that this is some sort of post mortem, we must stress at once that from an historical point of view the post-war monetary system has worked extraordinarily well. It took perhaps seven years to repair the damage of the greatest conflict that the world has ever known. Compare that with previous experience: the Thirty Years War laid waste central Europe for a century and more; and the First World War was followed by massive unemployment, by economic stagnation, and by currency collapse. By contrast, since World War II most of the developed countries have managed real growth rates of around 4 per cent a year. Some, like Japan, have achieved much more. We may complain that Britain has done badly by only growing at 2½–3 per cent. But that rate of growth is probably higher than at any time in her history. Even in the heady days of the Industrial Revolution, taking boom and slump years together, the growth rate averaged little more than 2 per cent.

This unparalleled world prosperity cannot be attributed entirely to the success of the international payments system. There are many other factors too. The larger share of resources going into industrial investment rather than consumption, the increasing speed of technical advance, and the greater knowledge of how to control and stimulate economics are among them. Yet the boom in world trade since the war has been a vital feature of economic recovery, just as the depression in trade was at the centre of the collapse of the 1930s. And this boom can at least in part be attributed to the work of Bretton Woods. Since the last war the annual increase in world trade has been running at between 6 and 7 per cent a year; that is, faster than the increase in world production. Indeed one of the most remarkable things is the way that this growth has been

128

speeding up in recent years, despite the international money problem. In 1968 world trade leapt 11 per cent in value—close to an all-time record. It was not until 1950 that world trade got back to the level it had reached in 1929 (measured in volume). But since then it has bounded ahead, and now stands, taking exports and imports together, at close on $500,000 million a year.

So the system has succeeded in its main object—at any rate so far. But there have been increasing signs of strain, especially during the 1960s. Crises and shocks have struck at the core of the prosperity of the post-war era. We must, therefore, try to sort out what has been going wrong and why; and what can be done about it.

Let us start with the main events. The post-war period can be split into three distinct phases. To start with, until about 1958 the picture was one of steady progress towards freedom of trade and of currencies. There were problems and setbacks, of course, like the failure of the first attempt to restore sterling convertibility in 1947. But the fundamental assumption on which the whole edifice was raised—the continuing dominance of the US economy and of the dollar—remained unchallenged.

In fact a precise date can be put to the end of this period. It was December 27, 1958, when all major European currencies finally became fully convertible to external holders (that is, foreign holders of, say, Italian lire could freely exchange them for French francs). But in reality it was the changed relationships between Europe and America that brought it to a close. And this was a more gradual process.

After 1958 the results of post-war reconstruction in Europe began to make their mark on the international monetary front. European countries had become competitive and were soon building up their gold reserves just when the United States was moving into deficit and losing gold. And it was at this time that the six common Market countries came to realize the long-term effects of the continuing US payments deficit. With some justification they felt that the United States was able to use her position as a reserve currency to run a payments deficit longer than other nations, and thus to build up her investments

I   129 in Europe and to pursue a world role of which European governments, particularly the new French regime of General de Gaulle, did not necessarily approve.

Thus from 1958 to the mid-1960s the world monetary scene was dominated by this shift of monetary power from the US to Europe and by the repercussions of increasing currency freedom. Money could move freely round the world again and, as a result, started to create new problems. It began to move in very large amounts. So when a series of crises cropped up in the early 1960s they were marked by large speculative flows of funds between currencies and, although there was little that could be done to stop the flows, for a while they were at least contained by international co-operation.

By 1964—the start of our third period—it had become increasingly apparent that international co-operation alone would not be able to shore up the system for much longer. The pressures on individual currencies were increasing with each crisis. More radical solutions seemed to be needed. But before we attempt to describe them, it may be useful to summarize the main features of these three post-war periods.

1945–58: Moves towards Freer Trade and Freer Currencies
First the economic recovery of Europe was fostered by American and, to a lesser extent, Canadian loans. When these appeared inadequate the massive Marshall Aid[1] programme of the US was introduced. This injection of capital was followed in the early 1950s by a gradual removal of barriers both to trade and to currency movements, leading to increasing prosperity and full employment. This period ended on December 27, 1958, when, as we have indicated, all major currencies (including sterling) became convertible for non-residents. Yet throughout the 1950s there had been a troublesome dollar shortage, while successive sterling crises had already shown some potential instability in the system.

1958–64: Results of Freer Currencies—Need for Co-operation
This instability grew very much worse in the next decade. The

[1] Marshall Aid to Europe between 1948 and 1952 totalled $13,812 million.

130

US had been running sizeable payments deficits in the late 1950s. But because of the dollar shortage inherited from the war, Europe was happy to hold her currency. After 1958 a change took place. The formation of the Common Market had begun to stimulate the economies of the major European powers, Germany, France and Italy. The strength of these economies, plus the increasing deficit of the United States, led to a transfer of reserves from America to Europe. European holdings of dollars mounted and their central banks began to switch them into gold and, as a result, the gold reserves of the US were slowly reduced. In addition the large movements of short-term funds, now possible because of convertibility, led to a series of currency crises: a gold crisis in 1960, a German mark crisis in 1961 and a sterling crisis in the same year. To start with these flows were managed by international co-operation. The gold pool stabilized the free market price of gold, central bank 'swaps' were developed to counteract international money flows, the Bank for International Settlements took on a new significance as a forum for co-operation and debate, and the IMF gradually increased its lending. Yet by the late 1960s it became clear that these efforts would not be enough to maintain stability.

1964 Onwards: Deeper Crises—Need for Solutions
The forces that led to the imbalances of the early 1960s grew worse. There was a continuing shift in economic power from the United States to Europe. The US gold reserve continued to fall. The immediate reaction of the US authorities was to try to get Europe to hold more dollars. But the US was faced with the implacable opposition of General de Gaulle. France converted her increasing dollar surpluses into gold and even insisted on that gold being shipped to France. The French opposition to monetary reform (except a return to gold) was growing just when a succession of sterling crises—from November 1964 onwards—was starting to shake the system to its foundations. Matters came to a head with the sterling devaluation of 1967. Until then the façade could be maintained that the reserve currencies were as good as gold. Once sterling

131

had fallen attention focused on the dollar. A few short months afterwards, in March 1968, a run into gold began. Because the dollar price of gold had been one of the fundamentals of the post-war system this was in reality an attack on the dollar. Though this crisis was again staved off, this time by introducing a 'two-tier' price structure for gold, the uncertainties remained. Devaluation of the French franc and revaluation of the mark followed in 1969.

Such, in a nutshell, are the main monetary landmarks of the first two decades after the war. We can now try to extract some of the main forces at work and a few lessons.

1. *Inflation*

Though all these phases were periods of high prosperity, at any rate for the developed world, they were also periods of inflation. This was not the socially destructive galloping inflation of Germany in the 1920s. Rather it was a creeping, almost unnoticeable, reduction of the buying power of money. From an internal point of view it apparently mattered little except that certain sections of the community benefited at the expense of others. If all countries had inflated at the same rate it would have mattered little for the international exchange system too. But they didn't. And this disequilibrium has been shown to be incompatible with fixed exchange rates. Thus though the German mark has declined in value by an average 2·2 per cent a year over the last ten years and the United States dollar by a mere 1·9 per cent, currencies like the French franc have averaged a loss of nearly 4 per cent of their value every year. For some South American countries the picture becomes ridiculous. Several countries now find their currencies worth less than half what they were even five years ago. Any fixed parity system must find it difficult to work under these circumstances. The scope for speculative movements of capital to take advantage of impending devaluations is obvious.

2. *Speculation*

As we have explained, this is simply a matter of taking advantage of events or trying to find protection against them. Accordingly, post-war events provided the motive and the increasing freedom of capital and trade provided the opportunity. Both led to large flows of short-term funds.

3. *Trade Imbalance between Nations*

But speculation was only one way in which the varying rates of inflation led to instability. A more fundamental reason was quite simply that some countries found that their goods were becoming more and more competitive in world markets. And vice versa. Germany is the best example of increasing competitiveness. Despite one revaluation of the mark (in 1961), export surpluses mounted up, reaching $5,700 million in 1968. This trade surplus, which can be ascribed largely to the low rate of inflation in Germany, was the major factor leading to the second revaluation of the mark in the autumn of 1969. This sort of situation had been anticipated by the planners of Bretton Woods in 1944. If a country was to get into substantial payments surplus or deficit no one denied that there was a case for revaluing or devaluing its currency. But what they did not appreciate was how often such an imbalance might develop. Worse, some of these imbalances were not the result of trade at all, but sometimes because of other factors such as government transactions (defence spending abroad, aid etc.). This possibility was not appreciated at Bretton Woods.

4. *Other Imbalances*

Taking visible and invisible trade accounts together, both the UK and the US have generally been in persistent surplus since the war. Yet both have had severe balance of payments problems, with both sterling and the dollar under pressure. Until 1969 at any rate it was ridiculous to claim that the US was uncompetitive. Throughout the 1950s and 1960s she had a trade surplus of $2,000–3,000 million a year. It rose to nearly $7,000 million in 1964. On top of this there was income from investments, from financial services and other 'invisible' sources. Yet throughout the 1960s she was running an overall balance of payments deficit of around $2,000–3,000 million. This deficit was caused by US investment abroad, military expenditure, and

133

foreign aid—all items which might be loosely termed part of America's role in the world.

Britain does not present quite the same picture. Whereas it was only in 1968 that the US trade surplus was eroded and the economy began to look less competitive, there has been concern ever since the war about Britain's ability to pay her way. But again the idea that it is a trade imbalance that is at the root of her balance of payments problems is at best misleading, at worst quite wrong. Very briefly, if Britain's balance of payments is analysed it can be seen that since the war she has not been in deficit on her private transactions. If her persistent surplus on invisible income is added to her trade balance (which is more often than not in deficit) the total not only comes out in surplus, but there is quite a bit left over to pay for things like foreign investment. What there was not enough left over for during the second half of the 1960s was military spending abroad and aid—hence one of the major causes of Britain's problems between 1964 and 1968.

5. *Rigidities in the System*

We have just described some of the pressures on the system. Had it been a more flexible one, it might have been able to cope. But two important rigidities have continuously harassed the efforts of central bankers to keep it going.

(*a*) *The problem of changing exchange rates.* The reasons why rates have to change should be clear. But how can it be done without encouraging speculation? The main problem is that under the IMFs rules (designed to prevent too many changes) a whole set of national values has often become attached to exchange rates. There is no philosophical, religious or moral reason why an exchange rate of $2.80 to the £ is better or worse than one of $2.40. Equally there is no reason why $2.40 is better or worse than say $2.45. But such is the fixed parity system that countries tend to think of an exchange rate as something to be protected at all costs, often from purely patriotic pride. This has encouraged delays in devaluations and revaluations, making the event all the more cataclysmic when it did arrive.

(*b*) *The problem of the fixed gold price.* The price of gold has been fixed in terms of the US dollar at \$35 per fine ounce since 1934. During this time the prices of all the goods in world trade have doubled, trebled, or in some cases, increased tenfold. In addition to this, the volume of world trade has bounded ahead. So there are two quite separate forces pushing up the price of gold. Yet, and here the problem links with the rigidity of exchange rates, such is the prestige attached to the gold price that it would be thought of as a devaluation of the dollar if the price were to be changed. The US has stoutly resisted all efforts to revalue gold.

6. *The Crises*
The result of these pressures moving against these rigidities is what part of this book is about: the set of crises that beleaguered the world during the 1960s and which have continued to threaten the post-war boom. Invariably they centre round one or other of the major currencies.

(*a*) *Sterling.* Sterling has for long periods been the weak link of the whole system. We explained earlier why it is a reserve currency and in theory can be changed into gold on demand. We have also talked about the sterling balances—sterling in foreign hands—that can be presented for payment at the Bank of England. Whenever people become worried about the international money system they want gold and other more stable currencies, and sterling is a convenient way of acquiring them. Britain's own difficulties in balancing her payments have added to the problem. So in 1955, in 1957, 1961, 1964, 1966, 1967, 1968 and 1969 there were the runs into gold and into marks, none of which were directly concerned with Britain's domestic position. Each of these runs (apart from 1967 when Britain was forced to devalue) was 'beaten' by international co-operation.

(*b*) *The mark.* The German mark has twice come into particular prominence. Formed out of the rubble of occupied Germany, it has since earned a position as the strongest currency in the world. The reason is not hard to see. Twice in living memory Germany has been struck by bounding inflation

135

and had to resort to a cigarettes currency (i.e. goods have become more *useful* than currency). As a result post-war German governments have made the stability of the mark a top priority of economic policy—and the resultant competitiveness has plainly helped to build up a continuous trade surplus. On top of this there have been substantial injections of foreign exchange from NATO troops stationed in Germany. So by the end of the 1950s it had become clear that the mark was overvalued in terms of the currencies of its main trading partners, and a 5 per cent revaluation was agreed to by the German authorities in 1961. Looking back it is clear that this was not enough. The trade surpluses continued, indeed grew, while Germany remained reluctant (or unable) to invest abroad most of the funds it had been accumulating. It preferred instead to add to its foreign reserves which mounted from $7,000 million in 1960 to nearly $10,000 million at the end of 1968. Ten months later the mark was revalued for the second time.

(*c*) *The franc.* The franc was a problem currency throughout the 1950s. In the years from 1945 to 1958 it was devalued no less than five times. But curiously it was not until it achieved stability that it started to cause headaches for the international monetary authorities. Stability came in 1958 with the reign of General de Gaulle when, for the first time, a franc devaluation was accompanied by stiff domestic measures. With the franc consequently undervalued France was able during the early 1960s to run a series of payment surpluses. The growth of inter-Common Market trade helped. She was also helped by the fact that she had been forced to scale down her overseas commitments, and that almost all her foreign aid was to countries in the franc area and so did not drain her reserves. As a result she was able to build up her reserves mainly at the expense of the US. But, unlike Germany, she carried out a specific policy of converting all her payment surpluses into gold. Such a policy was killed, as was the Gaullist regime, by the events of 1968. Devaluation followed little more than a year later.

(*d*) *The dollar.* And so to the central problem. Many of the difficulties raised by this leading world currency must already be clear. It never occurred to the planners of 1944 that the

136

dollar would come under suspicion. Still less that the link with gold would become little more than a façade. Yet both have happened. The gold crisis in the spring of 1968 was really a crisis of confidence in the dollar. It must be remembered that sterling had been devalued only six months before. The repeated denials of any revaluation of the dollar value of gold by the US authorities seemed for a while as valueless as those of the UK Government a few months earlier. Nothing seemed sacred. The US gold stock had slumped to little over $10,000 million from a level of over $26,000 million ten years earlier. The run on gold started. The US, as a major contributor to the gold pool (the club of central banks that kept the free market price of gold close to $35 an ounce by buying and selling around that price), decided that it had had enough. And the two-tier gold system was introduced. The idea behind this was simple. While the $35 price would be kept for international settlements purposes, the market price would be allowed to rise or fall freely. On the face of it all this was really doing was going back to the days before the gold pool started to operate. But there were two important differences. Firstly, everyone had got used to the idea of the gold price being maintained at one level. Such a move represented a major blow to confidence in the system. Secondly, the US no longer undertook to *buy* gold at the official price. Before, she had always done so. The importance of this was that the bottom peg to the price of gold no longer existed. And by the early part of 1970 the official price had dropped below $35, though it rose again later.

Having thus outlined some of the major forces and issues of the post-war years, we must now turn to the final question: what can be done? We set out the various theoretical possibilities of a world money system in an earlier chapter. One way out would be to overthrow the present rigid system and introduce a new one, with floating rates, for example, instead. But, as we have seen, such a solution would hardly commend itself to central bankers and governments. We must, therefore, look briefly at the practical possibilities, at the ways in which present arrangements can be modified without throwing the baby out with the bath water. First we look at the adjustment problem.

1. *More Co-operation*

Already central banks have become accustomed to devising schemes to counter speculative flows of money across frontiers. The Basle credits for sterling noted in Chapter 6 are a good example. The recycling of funds, e.g. the returning of money from German to other hands such as happened during the mark crisis in 1969, is another. These kind of arrangements could be taken further so that all speculative movements might be isolated. Then countries could carry out their domestic policies without fear of being blown off course by the speculators. But this is only one side of international co-operation. The process of lending more money to countries in payments difficulties will only cure speculation. If there is a flaw in the borrower's economic policies leading to a balance of payments deficit, borrowing will do no more than stave off the evil day. What is needed is greater use of 'surveillance'—the term used by international bodies examining and advising national governments on what policies they should pursue. At present the IMF keeps a pretty tight rein on countries that borrow from it. Such surveillance could be increased and extended. Or it could be if countries would agree to it.

2. *More Flexibility*

We have argued that a major trouble with the present system is its inflexibility: that when changes in exchange rates come they are too drastic and too sudden; sometimes too late. There are two ways in which the system could be modified:

(*a*) *Wider bands*. At present under IMF regulations countries have to keep their currencies within 1 per cent either side of the parity. If this were increased to say 5 per cent then speculation could become a much more hazardous exercise. The potential losses for the speculators would be much greater.

(*b*) *Crawling peg*. The idea behind this is that instead of a fixed exchange rate as at present, the exchange rate would be allowed to move very slowly (say by one per cent a year) up

138

or down. This system could, if desired, be combined with wider bands to give many of the advantages of a floating exchange rate without so many of the dangers.

3. *Changes in Reserves*
Changes could also take place in the constituents of gold and exchange reserves. The problem falls into three parts.

(*a*) *Gold.* Everyone agrees that something has to be done, that the present price structure is artificial and cannot be trusted for long. There is a fundamental decision to be made whether we want gold to remain at the centre of the monetary system or not. If the answer is 'yes' then we may have to be prepared to let the gold price rise to its market level. At present this is politically difficult, though it is always worth remembering that if the whole system does break down we will probably be forced to return to the sole use of gold for international payments, and at a very much higher price than at present. The other option is to get rid of gold entirely. It seems an insult to someone's intelligence to spend time and effort digging the metal out of the ground only to hoard it in the vaults of a central bank. Although it may be pretty to look at and to wear, and may be useful in coating lunar modules, has it (or should it have) any fundamental monetary use? To ask this question is to go back to Chapter 1 and to the basic question: what is money all about? While it may seem logical, therefore, to get rid of gold, the success of any such move will fundamentally depend on the beliefs of individuals. Because if enough people really believe in gold and have greater faith in it than in their own currencies, gold is bound to retain its value.

(*b*) *Reserve currencies.* Whatever happens to gold, something will have to be done about the two reserve currencies, the pound and the dollar. One solution is to transfer the responsibility for them from the nations concerned to some supra-national body. The pound and the dollar can and doubtless will continue to be essential to oil the wheels of world trade. But this is a separate matter from being held as reserves. In the case of sterling the transfer would now be relatively easy. Britain's debts are already in the form of international loans as well as

139

in sterling balances to national holders. An international funding operation could technically be mounted, were there the will to do so. In the case of the dollar the problem seems more difficult to solve given present attitudes. In short the US is not going to transfer dollar balances to an international body. The best we can hope for is that it will be forced to stop adding to its liabilities.

(c) *New world money.* This is what the world's finance ministers put into operation at the IMF conference of 1969. They called the money Special Drawing Rights or SDRs, but in effect it is a new IMF currency. Just how it works is described in Chapter 18. Here we shall simply note some of the problems SDRs (or any new world money) are likely to run up against.

In the first place, would such a new currency be generally acceptable? We have seen that acceptability is perhaps the most important feature of money. SDRs have yet to prove themselves in a crisis. Secondly, how much new money should be created in future, after the initial creation for 1970–72? Who is going to decide? What happens if a large number of countries get worried about the amount that is being created and demand gold instead? Again we are taken back to the first chapter and the question 'What is money for?' The IMF does not have the sovereign power of a national government. It cannot tax individuals, so it cannot redeem SDRs in real goods. We may find that the only way world money can be created on any significant and lasting scale is to have a world government. And until then?

HOW IT WILL WORK

Chapter 14

WILL 1929 RECUR?

*Some years, like some poets and politicians and some
lovely women, are singled out for fame far beyond the
common lot, and 1929 was clearly such a year. Like 1066,
1776, and 1914, it is a year that everyone remembers. One
went to college before 1929, was married after 1929, or
wasn't even born in 1929, which bespeaks total innocence.
A reference to 1929 has become shorthand for the events of
that autumn. For a decade, whenever Americans have been
afflicted with doubt as to the durability of their current
state of prosperity, they have asked 'Will it be 1929 all
over again'.*
—J. K. Galbraith, *The Great Crash, 1929.*

*The United States is in the midst of the worst financial
crisis since 1931. We are faced with an intolerable Budget
deficit, and also an intolerable deficit in our international
balance of payments. Both have to be corrected over the
next few years if the United States is going to face either
an uncontrollable recession or an uncontrollable inflation.
Unless we reverse our current trend it will inevitably lead
to world-wide devaluation of currency and that would be
the greatest setback this country has faced in my lifetime.
It would take us a long time to recover.*
—William McChesney Martin, Chairman, Federal
Reserve Board, April 20, 1968

The United States is reliving the dismal history of 1929.
—J. K. Galbraith, May 1970.

143

Could 1929 and what it means in terms of world economic and financial disaster ever happen again? This question has been asked several times since the war in 1962, 1963, 1968 and particularly, 1970. The straightforward answer is that history never repeats itself. There is little or no comparison between the conditions in the world today and the events following the 1914–18 war. The bankers, economists, the businessmen, the man in the street, and the politicians are all wiser, better informed, more flexible in their attitudes and better equipped mentally and materially.

Yet it would be foolhardy to suggest that the Western nations are secure from world-wide financial trouble, crises, devaluations and unemployment. Even if history may sometimes seem to repeat itself, most of us would like to add, 'at least the pattern is never exactly the same'.

In spite of our great advance in economic knowledge and the increased skills of central bankers and treasury officials, many people still feel that there is something odd about money. The international monetary arrangements which are set up after long or sudden consultation are often so highly complicated. At the same time, the system itself seems to be so easily endangered by the most irrational actions: a flight from money, a run on the pound (franc, dollar, mark, etc.), a crisis of confidence. The suspicion lingers that there are still some odd quirks in this world of money, some of which might backfire and bring disaster.

Then there are the 'where are we all going?' sort of questions. As economies grow richer they grow faster. In the United States, the increase each year in the gross national product alone is equal to the whole of the gross national product of a country like Ireland. Something like compound interest seems to step in with the increases becoming larger each year. Someone has to buy these extra goods. Is the human consumer really insatiable?

There are plenty of poor countries, of course, but these are not the areas which are growing. It is in the US, Germany, and Japan where, if recent rates of growth are maintained, the question might one day arise of whether consumers in these

144

countries can be persuaded to buy more and more of what in terms of basic human needs they no longer really require.

The rich nations must sell their goods abroad and export their capital to keep their economies at full production. But how are the poorer nations to find the means of payment? Is this in the long-term where the new crash may come?

These are some of the questions that come to mind in considering where the next threat to world prosperity may arise. We can in fact be more specific and put our finger on three sensitive spots in the world economy—areas that have proved vulnerable before and may do so again:

(a) The financial markets (the repercussions of the stock markets and the actions of the leading commercial banks).

(b) The trend of economic activity (production and consumption) in leading countries.

(c) The movements of world currencies.

These three areas—the legislation which controls them, government action within them, the role of international organizations and the attitudes held by the man in the street—are the main threats to world prosperity.

In this chapter we take another look at what actually occurred in 1929 to see whether in the technical and historical breakdowns which brought about the Great Depression there are similarities with the present situation. Then we will ask if the fantastic could really happen, whether a surfeit of too much worldly wealth could produce a paucity.

Seen in narrow stock market terms, the first sensitive spot, there is no doubt that the mathematics of 1929 are repeatable. It is the New York stock exchange which throws up the really dramatic figures because of its size, the volatile nature of its trading and the records of turnover available. Historically, in any case, '1929' started in America—which still remains the most powerful of the Western economies. 'When Wall Street sneezes the rest of capitalism catches cold' is an adage which still holds true.

There have been several days in recent history outstanding for the size of the stock market losses—Black Tuesday, October 29, 1929; Black Monday, May 28, 1962; and Black Friday, November 23, 1963. It really matters little which in numerical terms established the record drop. The key factor is the length of time the depression lasted. After the 1929 crash the index of common stocks which stood at 225 in September 1929 (1926=100) had reached 32 by June 1932. The crisis of 1929 was the beginning of a long and continuous decline and not a sudden ephemeral day of panic as Black Monday and Black Friday fortunately both turned out to be.

So far as statistics are concerned May 1962 and 1970 have come nearest to producing figures approaching the situation of 1929. After President Kennedy's action to prevent a rise in steel prices the total number of shares traded on May 28, 1962, was 9,350,000 the largest number sold since 1933 and slightly greater than the volume reached on October 29, 1929. On the following day the record of 16,410,030 was sold. The Dow Jones index on Monday, May 29, 1962, dropped 35 points but regained 27 of these points the next day.

In the two hours after the news of President Kennedy's assassination on Friday, November 23, 1963, and before dealings were suspended the Dow Jones index fell 21 points. The market remained closed but when it was reopened the following day Tuesday, November 26th, this loss was more than made good by a gain of 32·03 points, the largest increase on record—until a 32·04 gain on May 27, 1970.

Before 1929 the New York stock exchange was relatively uncontrolled and not the heavily policed, highly regulated institution of today. Not only had the speculation of the 1920s brought highly suspect companies to the market, but also a few which did not appear to exist at all. Yet none lacked eager investors, and it was said that the more speculative the prospectus, the heavier the over subscription. Speculators borrowed money at 10 per cent to buy shares that earned 2 per cent at current prices.

Because many of these shareholdings had been financed by credit (that is, 'bought on margin') a chain reaction followed the initial fall. To finance the purchase of the more worthless

146

equities good shares had to be sold. This, in turn, caused the share prices of profitable companies to slump producing a need for further sales of equities. The snowball effect eventually endangered the working capital of efficiently run companies and caused them to cut back production, cancel capital expenditures, and dismiss workers.

The stock exchange was only a part, if a highly dramatic part, of that sensitive spot called the financial markets. In several Western countries the banking system broke down quite as completely as the stock markets and bourses. Here too a chain reaction brought bankruptcies in its wake. In the spring of 1931, the Kreditanstalt, Austria's largest bank, suspended payments. The panic quickly spread to Germany where, in July 1931, the Norddeutsche Wollkammerei in Bremen failed; bringing down also its largest creditor, the Darmstadter und Nationalbank.

In March 1933, all American banks were closed and only allowed to reopen gradually as they showed they could meet their obligations. In Britain alone was there no run on the banks.

As with the stock market crash, the banking upheaval was followed by government action in the form of legislation. In the US this meant the strengthening of the Federal Reserve system to regulate the flow of credit and so exercise control over business activity. Other countries took similar steps and in many it was the first time that central banks were brought fully under government authority.

Vast though the amount of legislation has been since 1929, and important though this has been in giving protection against similar disasters, the key factor lies in the complete change in the orthodox attitude towards unemployment. No longer is the existence of enormous armies of unemployed looked upon as akin to an act of God about which nothing can (or should) be done. No longer is the capitalist system seen as self-correcting with business cycles and depressions part of a natural order.

The notion that economic insecurity is essential to progress and efficiency was a major miscalculation. A healthy economic and financial climate is now seen as necessary for investment in new technology, proper planning, and the efficient working of business.

We have been examining what might be called the technical areas which proved vulnerable in 1929—the stock markets and the repercussions on the domestic banking scenes. The expertise required to make these markets function efficiently seemed to demand a price in unemployment and poverty in some sections of the community which it was impossible to pay. The *laissez-faire* system had been questioned.

And so on to the second of our sensitive spots: the trend of economic activity. Very largely thanks to Lord Keynes, the inter-relation between demand and production is more clearly understood. From 1936, when he launched his formal assault in the *General Theory of Employment Interest and Money*, a system of thought has been available to tackle the problem of unemployment. In the United States, the total of unemployed rose from 429,000 in 1929 to nearly 12 million in 1933, out of a labour force of 48 million. At the end of 1932, in the extreme case of Germany 43 per cent of the labour force was out of work. For all Western Europe, unemployment rose from 3,500,000 in the period 1921 to 1925 to a seasonal peak of 15,000,000 at the end of 1932.

And yet, in spite of these figures, this was still the era of the annually balanced budget. Instead of increasing government expenditure to keep people employed and demand up, cuts were made in public projects because, with business activity slack, revenue from taxation fell, and so, with a smaller income, the governments had less to spend. This was the dogma, though, in practice, from 1930 onwards few national budgets were ever balanced again.

The Keynesian theory of aggregate demand would today bring in programmes of public works, tax relief on businesses and deficit budgetary finance. There is, moreover, a built-in stabilizing effect in the unemployment benefits, old-age pensions and the different allowances now made under welfare state legislation.

On the other hand, it would be foolish to ignore the fact that, were a lasting depression to occur, the above measures would probably still be inadequate. Threatened by a drastic loss of markets, businessmen would return to cut-throat price competition. Unemployment benefit then becomes not a transitional protection for a worker between jobs but an inadequate living wage. Other support prices like those in agriculture change from being high minimums to low maximums. We must not pretend that the present economic system has become the self-correcting mechanism the old one was supposed to be.

Having apparently gone a long way towards solving the unemployment problem, the industrial countries now face a new task of combating inflation. And, although public choices may change, electorates at present have clearly decided that they prefer inflation to unemployment. While governments may still call for sacrifices—a politician's reaction to any problem—it is now unlikely they would (or could) actually insist on the sort of sacrifices demanded in the 1930s.

There remains the international currency scene, the third sensitive spot on the world economy which may again prove vulnerable. Many of the causes leading up to the 1929 disaster were explained in Chapter 2. Aspects of the 1929 crash examined so far—stock market crash, bankruptcies, bank failures and massive unemployment—have led us to follow the events of 1929 forward into the 1930s, more or less up to the outbreak of the Second World War. To explain the world trading situation, we must go back to the end of the First World War.

It is in the run up to 1929 that the similarities with today's economic situation might be regarded as most striking. Germany ended the First World War impoverished and loaded down with reparation payments which had to be made to the victorious nations.

These payments were met initially by simply borrowing from abroad. Between 1924 and 1930 American and other foreign bankers granted Germany countless loans. In addition, German banks were also borrowing abroad short-term with much of these funds being used for stock exchange speculation. Within six years (1923 to 1929) Germany had borrowed 20 billion marks from abroad—as much as the US had used for its development over the previous forty years! Of course, these debts went unpaid. After various repayment schemes and international conferences the Hoover moratorium in 1931 ended an impossible situation.

149

The placing of these loans had, however, been highly profitable for New York and London bankers in the early 1920s. It was, in fact, part of the frenzied speculation that was to lead up to the Wall Street crash.

It would be easy, though totally misleading, to point to similar activities in new issue markets over the past ten years or so. True maintenance of New York and London as leading world capital markets has been due to the resourcefulness of its bankers. In a world of restrictions on capital movements, great ingenuity is shown by bankers in devising new forms of money raising which circumvent Treasury or central bank controls. This is in the nature of the banking business which must be internationally orientated. If government action prevents the bankers from performing their functions in one way they will find another. Moreover, as with any legal system when it becomes either too restrictive or too complicated for easy interpretation or both it tends to fall into disrepute. Loopholes are found and become socially acceptable.

The German reparation payments may have been unjust; they were certainly wildly unrealistic in financial and economic terms. German bankers might therefore have considered themselves not too morally involved in what followed. In any case, the central banking authorities at that time had quite inadequate powers to control the situation.

In contrast, the control of central banks today over their national finances in their individual countries could hardly be more complete. But, perhaps like generals fighting battles, the central bankers are enforcing the solutions of previous monetary crises. To some extent, because of the rigid controls now enforced, new money markets have been created beyond the control of individual national entities. The vast eurodollar market (discussed in some detail in Chapter 20) truly international in character, is fulfilling this function. It is needed because industry is becoming increasingly international. The supranational giants, the major oil and shipping concerns require world-wide finance. The scale of world trade has grown dramatically and so have capital requirements.

These huge international funds cannot be controlled by

individual national institutions, as recent speculative raids on various currencies have shown. The pound has been in the forefront of these raids because of Britain's persistent payments deficit. But the very large sums which Britain borrowed from the IMF and other central banks are in no way comparable with the German debts of the 1920s and 1930s. In the first place, the UK owns more than enough foreign securities and direct investment abroad to cover the loans. Secondly, Britain's position as an advanced, highly industrialized nation has little in common with the impoverished and demoralized Germany of the 1920s.

Of course, the biggest ground of all for hope and the most significant difference between today and the 1920s has been the effective consultation between the leading nations of the world in monetary crises. Nor have the steps forward towards freer trade between countries been eroded. When Germany in the 1930s attempted to achieve an export surplus to earn the foreign exchange to make the reparation payments, it found a universal move to raise tariff barriers against its goods. So far the interdependence of world markets as buyers and sellers of each other's goods has been kept in the forefront of international discussions. And, as long as trade continues to flow, economic breakdowns can be avoided.

It might be useful to summarize the advances made in controlling economies since 1929:

1. Stock market legislation especially in the leading exchanges of New York and London has greatly increased the control over dealings and enlarged beyond recognition the amount of information which must be made available about all quoted companies.

2. The domestic banking systems in all major trading countries are now firmly under the guidance of governments.

3. Rules of inspection and creditworthiness make negligible the risks to depositors' money.

4. A highly sophisticated system of taxation, fiscal and monetary policy, of unemployment grants, old-age pensions, sickness benefits, government control of public works and nationalized industries all ensure attempts at keeping economies on an even keel.

151

5. On the international front world monetary co-operation has advanced to far frontiers.

6. Leading world central bankers discuss their problems each month at Basle, the meeting of the Bank for International Settlements.

7. For the world monetary system as a whole the International Monetary Fund supplies a system for overcoming critical situations and a forum for adjustments. (The working of the IMF is explained in Chapter 16.)

In addition to the crisis of confidence in financial markets, the failure to understand the consumer–producer relationship, and world currency scares there were a number of other events which at one time or another have been put forward as explanations for the 1929 crash. There are the non-recurring events peculiar to that age of development which do not fit into the three vulnerable areas which are always with us.

World War I brought about large-scale expansion of production with industry, especially in the US, geared to meet demands that could not be satisfied by an impoverished post-war Europe. Commodity supplies which had been greatly stimulated by wartime demands faced a price slump when the war ended. Moreover, the 1930s saw production rising as a result of a whole series of new processes from petroleum to plastics. Rationalization and standardization were introduced, and with it mass production began.

It was clearly a period of rapid technical change, but these developments took place against a background of disorganized and occasionally dishonest capital markets, a relatively unsophisticated banking system, and a rigid belief in *laissez faire*. Today things change much more rapidly than they ever did in the 1930s, but we have learned to accept change as part of our daily life, even to welcome it. So far, our staggering technological advances have not thrown world economies into chaos.

However, this suggests a bigger potential danger than ever the chancellors and economists of the 1930s failed to remove. It is the possibility that today we have become too good at producing things. Each year more and more is produced and

152

these products have to be consumed to avoid sparking off a slump—a deflationary cycle, to put the argument in its simplest, crudest terms.

The endemic unemployment of the 1930s was finally solved by Keynesian economics which recognized that what was produced in the aggregate had to be balanced by an aggregated demand. Otherwise, if demand was insufficient, goods would be left unsold; the companies making these goods would fail to make profits, cut back production and lay off workers. The latter would have less to spend and so still more goods would be left unsold. The circle is familiar.

Demand is kept at the necessary pitch to match production in many ways in a modern advanced society. All governments have large defence budgets, the advertising industry encourages new wants, obsolescence is contrived for goods long before their useful life is over. The onus, so runs the argument, is on the advertising and communications industries to create the desires for the goods which the manufacturers must produce.

The nightmare occurs, according to J. K. Galbraith, the author of *The Affluent Society*, when all the voices shouting their wares drown each other out. Modern business, he says, must manufacture not only goods but also the desire for the goods it manufactures. While production does not clearly contain within itself the seeds of its own disintegration, persuasion may:

'On some not distant day, the voice of each individual seller may well be lost in the collective roar of all together. Like injunctions to virtue and warnings of socialism, advertising will beat helplessly on ears that have been conditioned by previous assault to utter immunity.'

If this were to happen, the economic consequences could be momentous. Savings would immediately increase and, without compensating outlays, unemployment and depression could be expected to follow. Are the hippies and the drop-outs and the young people protesting against the consumer society the first signs?

153

This may seem to be carrying a theoretical possibility rather far, especially as Britain's standard of living is not only below that of the United States, but is now trailing behind that of Japan, Germany, Holland and Scandinavia as well.

There is also no evidence that the very rich in America find it harder to spend their money than anyone else. If they get tired of buying motor cars or television sets, or swimming pools, there is always gambling, works of art and alimony payments.

But if a small voice within you insists that there is a scale of values, that human beings do have a sense of priorities, then you may ask with Galbraith: why should life be made intolerable to make things of small urgency?

Certainly, the affluent society of today was unimagined in the 1930s. It is still beyond the imagination of the vast majority of the world's population. How the riches of the rich nations can be transferred to alleviate the poverty of the many poor nations is outside the scope of this book. Clearly, no solution has been found, nor is any answer in sight. If the human race has rarely responded to humanitarian pleas, self interest has proved a most powerful motive. And a fairer distribution of wealth throughout the world may be very much in our interests—if only to keep the machines turning.

Chapter 15

CAN GOLD BE REPLACED?

Thus gold, which was the major international reserve asset in the past, will continue to be held and used by monetary authorities. But its importance will gradually decline over time as S.D.R. supply the major part of reserve growth. This evolution, which recognizes the monetary importance of gold but avoids excessive dependence on it, seems to me to be the only rational course for the international monetary system to take.
—William McChesney Martin, Chairman, Federal Reserve Board, speaking to the National Industrial Conference Board in New York in March 1968.

If earlier chapters should have left the reader in little doubt about the central function of gold in the world's existing monetary system, it is equally fair to say that the role of gold in world payments is diminishing. In this chapter, therefore, we have to face two questions that may be vital to the world's future prosperity. (1) Can we get rid of gold in international payments? and (2) How can we replace gold?

If these questions had been asked ten years ago, the answers would have been quite different from many of those that follow. As the reader will already have realized two small, though significant, steps have already been taken towards replacing gold in international payments. The two-tier system, established in 1968, cut down the role of gold in payments between major nations. Secondly, the decision to issue $9,500 million of SDRs ('paper gold') over three years (1970–2) introduced a new method of international payment. We shall examine the implications in this chapter.

First we shall try to put the role of gold into perspective. We have already shown that gold is a relative newcomer to the international monetary system; that the sources of supply were extremely limited until just over a century ago; that although some gold coinage had been used since Greek and Roman times, until the nineteenth century most countries had used silver or copper for most or all of their currencies. It was not until the California gold rush of the 1840s, with the subsequent discovery of gold in Alaska, Russia, South Africa and Australia that gold became plentiful enough to oust silver. So the true gold standard actually existed for only about fifty years before the outbreak of World War I.

Britain was the first country to elevate the role of gold. By the late 1820s all barriers to the movement of gold had been gradually lifted, and transfers of gold were becoming more and more important in settling international debts. But until after 1870 not many other industrialized countries followed the British example. The United States did not abandon its bimetallic standard based on both gold and silver until 1893, and China, for example, never came off its silver standard.

By the time the Second World War broke out, most countries had moved onto an international gold exchange standard, which is what theoretically exists today. As we have already explained, under this system reserves are not held solely in gold. The close or even automatic relationship between the level of a country's reserves and the amount of domestic currency in circulation, which is a feature of a true gold standard, does not exist under an international gold exchange standard.

Gold, theoretically at least, remains the centre-piece of the gold exchange standard. To begin with, it still provides the largest single component of the published official reserves of the non-Communist world. At the end of 1969, there was known to be at least $38,920 million of gold in the vaults of the Western world's central banks, compared with total foreign exchange reserves of $30,940 million. Then again, gold is conventionally the standard in which members of the International Monetary Fund denominate their parity values. Moreover, the acceptability of sterling and dollars as international reserve currencies partly depended on their convertibility into gold. And finally, the new international reserve unit, the Special Drawing Rights,

156

will preserve links with the metal by being denominated in and closely tied to gold.

In recent years, however, a number of major changes have taken place in the international monetary system which have left the role of gold very much less important in practice than in theory. The changes began as the production of new gold progressively failed to keep pace with the rapid increase in private demand. In recent years, the production of new gold has risen slowly. The international price of the metal has been fixed by the US Treasury's willingness to buy gold at $35 a troy ounce, and this price has remained unchanged since 1934. Inevitably, it has become less economic to mine gold, and many marginal mines have been driven out of production. Between 1957 and 1966, about half of all newly mined gold went into the hands of private industry, speculators and hoarders; and in 1966, for the first time, all the year's gold production was absorbed by private demand.

The main source of new official reserves of world liquidity, in fact, over the last decade, has thus been not newly mined gold but reserve currencies and gold from the reserves of the United States. With the US running persistent balance of payments deficits, there has been a steady outflow of dollars to settle US debts with other countries. Some of these dollars found their way into official reserves and stayed there; others were cashed in with the US Treasury for gold at $35 an ounce.

This development had two effects on gold's role in international payments. First and most simply, it diminished the proportional importance of gold in the reserves of most countries. In 1950, gold holdings constituted more than two-thirds of the non-Communist world's reserves: by 1969, the proportion had fallen to just over a half.

Secondly, two classes of people exerted pressure for the price of gold to be raised. Those who were alarmed at the failure of world reserves to expand anything like as fast as the volume of world trade. And those who wanted an increase in the quantity of reserves but distrusted the various projects being canvassed for a new international reserve unit.

The efforts of these lobbies, led by France under General

157

de Gaulle, have so far proved abortive, but they draw attention to the fact that the value of gold was not, as General de Gaulle suggested, 'unalterable'. On the contrary, its price could be changed by the US Treasury acting with the consent of Congress. Indeed, far from the dollars being denominated in gold, gold was denominated in dollars. And it was on the strength of the dollar based on the enormous strength of the US economy, that the 'immutable' value of gold depended.

The establishment, in March 1968, of the two-tier gold market,[1] finally made it clear beyond all doubt that the world monetary system in practice revolved around the dollar rather than gold. Speculation on a change in the American gold price had risen rapidly throughout the previous year, and as gold poured out of the coffers of the Federal Reserve it became clear that the US would soon be faced with a choice between raising the price of gold—to increase the value of the metal in the reserves *vis-à-vis* the number of dollar bills in foreign hands—or refusing to sell gold at all.

After an emergency meeting of international bankers and finance ministers from Belgium, Italy, Germany, Switzerland, Netherlands, UK and the US in Washington DC, the US administration decided to compromise. It reached an agreement with the central banks of the major western nations, by which they undertook not to sell gold to private buyers. This agreement meant that the dollar became partly inconvertible into gold. Private individuals could no longer cash their dollars for gold either at their own central banks or at the US Treasury. It was also agreed, with some dissenters, that there was at present enough gold in official gold stocks.

Since the two-tier market was set up, the US has virtually suspended the conversion of dollars into gold even by central banks. This means that the most characteristic aspect of the gold exchange system no longer applies—namely, the major reserve currency is, understandably, no longer freely convertible. This policy change has not been spelled out by the US authorities in so many words. But, as Dr Milton Gilbert, of the Bank for International Settlements, said in April 1969, 'I find it hard

[1] Already described in Chapter 8 and also referred to in the previous chapter.

to believe the US Treasury would not reply "your judgement is different from ours" to any central bank which said it wanted gold'.

A second revolutionary outcome of the two-tier market agreement has been the virtual suspension of central bank purchases of newly mined gold from South Africa. Supplies of reserve gold had thus at least temporarily virtually dried up, with the two traditional sources the South African mines and the vaults of the Federal Reserve Bank, almost completely cut off.

This raises our second question. How can the world replace gold? As we have explained, international reserves will eventually be supplemented by adequate issues of Special Drawing Rights. Though frequently referred to by their nickname of 'paper-gold', these Special Drawing Rights have more in common with a reserve currency than with gold. The SDRs are, in fact, a new reserve asset created to ensure that sufficient international liquidity is available to finance the ever-growing volume of world trade; and to help countries with balance of payments problems to ride these out without throwing their trade with other countries into imbalance.

The amount of SDRs available to each member of the International Monetary Fund will depend on its quota in the Fund. For example, a Fund member whose quota is 1 per cent of total quotas would receive 1 per cent of any SDRs that may be allocated. Whilst the SDRs will be usable unconditionally, a country would only be expected to use them if it had a balance of payments problem or if the trends in its total reserves justified their use. As the SDRs will be carried in a special account of the IMF, they also need special financing. It is stipulated that each country participating in a given distribution of SDRs has to accept additional SDRs to a total of twice the amount of its allocation delivering convertible currencies against these additional SDRs. The surrender of these convertible currencies against the additional SDR allocation will help to finance the system. Finally, there are provisions for reconstituting the drawing rights, i.e. countries using their SDRs will incur an obligation to reconstitute their position. Exactly how the

159

SDR system will work is set out in some detail in Chapter 18. Here we are more concerned with the thinking which led to their creation and their likely effect on the world monetary system.

SDRS are a new concept; they are the first deliberate attempt to create reserves. For this reason they had to meet a number of requirements. They would be used purely for *international* reserve purposes. Unlike the dollar or sterling they would not bear the mark of any particular country, but instead would represent a claim against all the members of the IMF.

SDRS were also intended to be a final reserve asset, which meant that they could not be convertible into gold. At the same time they had to have a full gold guarantee so as to be accepted in co-existence with gold reserves. Again, they had to be a truly owned reserve with no strings attached and yet not be used for accentuating shifts from one kind of reserve to another.

Probably the most significant aspect of the SDR philosophy is that the volume of reserves created should be decided by international needs and not by the swings in any one country's balance of payments position or, for that matter, the vagaries of the gold market. This is certainly the view of West Germany's Dr Otmar Emminger, one of the architects of the SDR system. On the other hand, whilst some countries believe that supplementary reserves are needed to finance expanding world trade, in reality the reserves are not needed 'to finance world trade', but to solve deficits and surpluses of national balance of payments problems. Only a few weeks before the SDRS were activated by the IMF meeting in Washington in September 1969, Dr Emminger showed that whilst world trade between 1950 and 1968 had increased by an annual average of about $7\frac{1}{2}$ per cent, world reserves rose by only about $2\frac{1}{2}$ per cent annually. 'It is, however, noteworthy', he wrote, 'that during recent official discussions in the Group of Ten, no one suggested that in the coming years world reserves should necessarily be increased *pari passu* with the expected growth rate of world trade of about 8 per cent.'[1]

It has also been suggested that the creation of SDRS would automatically benefit countries like the US and Britain by help-

[1] *International Currency Review*, August 1969.

ing them to finance their present (or recent) deficits. Again, Dr
Emminger puts this into perspective. He feels the reverse would
be correct:

'For the whole purpose of the scheme has been to provide
supplementary reserves for the time when US deficits will have
largely disappeared and thus a major source of "traditional"
reserves will have dried up. Adequate supplies of reserves for the
rest of the world should help the US not to continue but to end
its chronic deficit.'

Another widespread criticism of the SDRs scheme has been
their automatic allocation. M. Jaques Rueff, the French
economist, has gone on record as saying 'gold is *earned* whereas
special drawing rights are *allocated*'. Which seems a surprising
argument for the arch-advocate of a doubling of the price of
gold as anything but a free gift to the holders of gold!

Whatever the future of the new reserve asset one thing is
clear: the approach is cautious. The initial allocation of SDRs
is unlikely to have more than a modest impact on the world
economy. Total world reserves stand at around $75,000 million.
The allocation of $9,500 million over a three-year period adds
only about 4 per cent each year and, what is more, the alloca-
tions are spread over a hundred countries.

Whilst we have tried to show that the adoption of the SDR
system marks a major milestone in world monetary affairs, it
would be both premature and facile to suggest that the SDRs
will be a cure-all or that in the next few years all major industrial
countries will cut loose from the tradition and mystique surrounding gold. Man's faith in gold is deep-rooted and on
occasions is likely to prove stronger than his confidence in his
fellow-men's ability to control economic affairs. Many countries have a large proportion of their official wealth tied up in
gold. Gold has played a vital role in an era of unprecedented
expansion and prosperity. In all likelihood, it will in co-
existence with SDRs play a significant part in any expansion of
the world monetary system. Taking a longer view, however, it
may not be unrealistic to foresee a day when the world will

L   161 have become sufficiently accustomed to 'artificial' reserve units and will replace much of the metal in central banking vaults with interest-earning book entries in the ledgers of the International Monetary Fund.

In the first chapter of this book we described its chief purpose: an attempt to explain the workings of the international monetary system in simple terms; to help those who are anxious to follow economic and monetary affairs to cut through the jargon which frequently clouds the issues. In the remaining chapters we try and explain how various international organizations, markets and specific operations work concluding with one on how to read the press; or rather of how to interpret the technical language that has inevitably crept into its financial columns.

Above all, however, we hope that this book will have shown that in spite of repeated monetary crises, in spite of devaluations and revaluations there are grounds for optimism that progress has been and is being made in man's quest for a more rational approach to world monetary affairs.

HOW EVERYTHING WORKS

Chapter 16

HOW THE IMF WORKS

(a) The Aims of the Fund
The purposes of the International Monetary Fund can best be understood from its own Articles of Agreement. These are, briefly, as follows:

1. To promote *international monetary co-operation* through a permanent institution which provides the machinery for consultation and collaboration on the world's monetary problems.

2. To facilitate the expansion and balanced *growth of world trade,* and to contribute to the promotion and maintenance of high levels of employment and real income and to the development of the productive resources of all members as primary objectives of economic policy.

3. To promote *exchange stability,* to maintain orderly exchange arrangements among members, and to avoid competitive exchange depreciation.

4. To assist in the establishment of a *multilateral system of* payments in respect of current transactions between members and in the elimination of foreign exchange restrictions which hamper the growth of world trade.

5. To give confidence to members by *making the Fund's resources* available to them under adequate safeguards, thus providing them with opportunity to correct maladjustments in their balance of payments without resorting to measures destructive of national or international prosperity.

6. In accordance with the above, to shorten the duration and *lessen the degree of disequilibrium* in the international balance of payments of members

(b) Brief History
These articles were drawn up at the international conference at Bretton Woods in New Hampshire in 1944. At that time a

number of international schemes were put forward with the aim both of setting a standard of good conduct in monetary affairs to guide governments, and of creating a new international body that would help countries live up to these ideals. The IMF emerged as a compromise between various plans.

The Fund came into operation on December 27, 1945, when it had thirty members. By the time of the 1969 annual report this had risen to 111: almost every country in the world outside the Communist bloc is now a member. Each country appoints a Governor, generally the head of its central bank or its finance minister, and an alternate governor, which gather at annual meetings to lay down policy. But day-to-day business is conducted by a board of executive directors, mostly based in Washington, headed by the managing director of the Fund.

To start with the work of the Fund was somewhat eclipsed by that of the World Bank (more properly the International Bank for Reconstruction and Development) formed at the same time. The work of the Bank seemed more pressing, first because Europe was still shattered economically, and later because of the need for development finance by the poorer nations. Besides, during the 1940s and early 1950s most currencies were protected by exchange controls and quota and tariff restrictions on trade. But, with the return to convertibility of most European currencies in 1958, the IMF came into its own.

The Fund's first function, the setting of a standard of conduct, has met a gradually increasing degree of success. Initially the parties set for major currencies were chosen on a rather arbitrary basis. By 1949 it became apparent that several were out of line and a massive set of devaluations was necessary. This was organized at the time of the fourth annual meeting. Since then there have been remarkably few parity changes of major industrial countries: apart from France, Britain has devalued once, the German mark has been revalued twice and the Canadian dollar has been allowed to float for a period. But by and large the aim of stable parities has been maintained. Beyond this there has been a gradual removal of barriers to the international movement of currencies, with all major currencies (more or less) convertible for non-residents since 1958.

166

In the early days borrowings were relatively small. There was a turning point in 1957. Until then the main borrowers tended to be relatively small countries, often in South America. Then the United Kingdom drew $1,300 million at the time of the Suez crisis, since when major countries—France and the United States as well as the UK—have increasingly used their borrowing facilities.

(c) How Borrowings are Financed
The principle on which the Fund operates is that countries can pay three-quarters of their quotas (or membership fees) in their own currency and one quarter in gold. In return countries can draw other people's currencies out. The Fund can only lend out money that it has already received.

Each country's quota varies roughly with its importance in world trade and payments. Both the overall size of the quotas and the relative size between different countries is changed from time to time, with the general agreement of the members. The last increase, early in 1970, raised members' total quotas to $24,000 million. To give an idea of the relative size of individual quotas, that of the UK is $2,800 million and that of the US is $6,700 million.

(d) How Money is Lent
A country in balance of payments difficulties can buy the foreign currency it needs from the Fund by offering more of its own currency, over and above its original subscription. These drawings from the Fund are available in different slices (known as 'tranches'). To start with the first 'gold tranche' can be drawn more or less automatically, that is, the borrowing country is given the benefit of any doubt about the reasons for the borrowing. After this, four additional tranches of up to 25 per cent each are available, which if fully drawn, would bring the Fund's holdings of a borrowing country's currency to 200 per cent of its quota. As the amount borrowed rises (especially beyond the first automatic 'gold tranche') the Fund takes an increasingly close interest in the country's economic policies, i.e. the bigger the borrowing the more substantial the justification required. Repayments are due within three to five years.

There is also a less formal form of borrowing, called stand-by arrangements, where the IMF grants short-term loans (usually for six months or a year) to help members get over purely temporary problems. Sometimes these stand-bys can be rolled over to give what is effectively longer-term credit.

Any country borrowing from the Fund within its credit tranches (i.e. beyond its 'gold tranche') or entering into a stand-by arrangement, is usually asked to explain in a 'letter of intent' the kind of economic policies it intends to pursue to put its economy in order again.

Chapter 17

HOW THE WORLD BANK WORKS

We have already shown that two complementary financial institutions emerged from the Bretton Woods Conference in 1944. The first, the IMF, was discussed in the previous chapter. The second institution, the International Bank for Reconstruction and Development, but better known as the World Bank was, as its name implies, created to help finance the reconstruction and development of its member countries.

Aims

It was realized that at the end of the war there would be a pressing need for international capital both to finance reconstruction, principally in Western Europe, and to increase productivity and living standards, especially in the underdeveloped areas of the world.

These requirements were recognized as being so great, and the risks of such a nature, that private capital would be unable to fulfill them without some form of government guarantee. Thus a new type of international investment institution was created which would be authorized to make guarantee loans for productive reconstruction and development projects both with its own capital funds and through the mobilization of private capital. Its financial structure was to be such that the risks of these investments would be shared by all member governments roughly in accordance with their economic strength.

Financial Structure

The Bank is an inter-governmental institution, corporate in form with all its capital stock owned by its member governments. The authorized capital was initially $10,000 million and is now equivalent to $24,000 million. Only one-tenth of this is paid in; the remaining 90 per cent may be called for by the

Bank if required to meet its obligations arising out of borrowings or guaranteeing loans.

The capital structure provides the Bank with substantial loan resources from its own paid-up capital and guarantees enable it to borrow even more sizeable resources, mainly through the sale of Bank obligations to private investors. The world's capital markets are the largest single source of funds. To the end of 1969 the Bank had raised the equivalent of $7,230 million by the sale of bonds and notes to investors.

Subscriptions by member countries to the Bank's capital stock are based on each member's quota in the IMF, which is designed to reflect the country's relative economic strength. Voting rights are related to shareholdings. Each member of the Bank has 250 votes plus one additional vote for each $100,000 of capital stock it subscribes. The Articles provide that, with certain exceptions, all matters before the Bank are decided by a majority vote.

Policy and Safeguards
It is one of the unique features of the Bank that, although it is an inter-governmental organization, it relies mainly upon private investors for its financial resources. This reflects the original concept of the Bank 'as a safe bridge over which private capital could move into the international field'.

To avoid errors of earlier international loan arrangements, the Bank's articles contain a number of protective provisions:

(*a*) The Bank's loans must be for high-priority productive purposes and, except in special circumstances, must be used to meet the foreign exchange requirements of specific projects of reconstruction or development;

(*b*) if the borrower is other than a government the loan must be guaranteed by the member government in whose territory the project is located, or by its central bank or some comparable agency;

(*c*) the Bank must act 'prudently' in making loans, paying due regard to whether the borrower or guarantor will be in a position to meet its obligation under the loan;

170

(*d*) the Bank is also specifically required to make arrangements to ensure that the proceeds of each loan are used only for the purpose for which the loan was granted and to pay attention to economy and efficiency.

There are three other important provisions governing the Bank's operations:

1. The Bank must be satisfied, before making any loan, that the borrower would be unable to obtain the loan from other sources on conditions reasonable for the borrower.
2. The Bank is prohibited from making 'tied' loans. This means it must not impose any conditions which require the proceeds of its loans to be spent in any particular member country or countries.
3. Only economic considerations should govern the Bank's decisions; it must not be influenced by the political character of the member or members concerned. By the same token the Bank and its officers must not interfere in the political affairs of any member.

Development Needs and Affiliates

Soon after the end of World War II it was found that the financial requirements for Europe's reconstruction far outstripped the resources of the World Bank. When the enlightened Marshall Plan proposals led to the European Recovery Programme (ERP) in 1948, the Bank turned its attention increasingly to its other major responsibility—the financing of development. This has remained its chief preoccupation. A high proportion of the Bank's loans since 1948 have been designed to provide basic services for the developing countries, e.g. power, roads, railways and harbours. More recently there has been growing emphasis on agriculture and education.

It became apparent too, before long, that there were gaps in the international financial structure which the World Bank could not fill. This led to the creation of two affiliated bodies, first the International Finance Corporation (IFC) and later the International Development Association (IDA).

171

International Finance Corporation
IFC came into being in 1956 to further economic development
by encouraging the growth of productive private enterprise in
developing member countries.

The Functions of IFC
   (*a*) IFC provides equity and loan capital for private enter-
prises in association with private investors and management;
   (*b*) encourages local capital markets;
   (*c*) stimulates the international flow of private capital; and
   (*d*) supports joint ventures which provide opportunities to
combine domestic knowledge of market and other conditions
with the technical and managerial experience available in the
industrialized countries.

As we have shown that the Bank's articles require it to obtain
a governmental guarantee for a loan to private enterprise.
Many governments are unwilling or unable to provide such a
guarantee, whilst many businessmen are reluctant to accept one.
Again, the Bank makes fixed-interest loans only and is not
authorized to subscribe to equity shares or provide other kinds
of risk capital. Hence the birth of the IFC.

International Development Association
IDA is the 'soft' loan arm of the World Bank. From the late
1940s onwards it became increasingly apparent that the developing countries were in need of external borrowing on cheaper
than conventional financial terms. This need was further
underlined in the early 1960s by the emergence of a large
number of newly independent countries in Africa who needed
development finance on concessionary terms. These countries
were no longer able to rely to the same extent on the financial
support of the metropolitan powers with whom they had been
associated. Nor had they developed sufficient credit standing of
their own to enable them to borrow on the scale they required.
Many newly independent states therefore became members of
the IDA which began its operations in 1960.
   IDA has extended development credits for a term of fifty

years, with an initial ten-year grace period and no interest charge, only a service charge of ¾ per cent. Loans provided on such uncommercial terms are known as 'soft' loans. Because it is impracticable for IDA to raise funds from private investors under these circumstances, IDA relies primarily on the governments of its richer member countries for its resources. As a result, IDA is persistently short of funds.

By mid-1969, the total funds made available to IDA amounted to $2,066 million, the bulk of which was accounted for by the initial subscriptions of member countries and a general replenishment in 1964.

Interlinked Membership

Only member countries of the International Monetary Fund may be considered for membership of the World Bank and membership of the Bank is a prerequisite for membership of both the IFC and IDA. Although legally and financially, IFC and IDA and the Bank are separate institutions, they are interlinked in many ways. The President of the Bank is *ex-officio* chairman of IFC's and IDA's Board of Directors and the Governors and Executive Directors of the Bank also serve on IFC and IDA if the countries which they represent are members of both institutions. IFC draws upon the Bank for administrative and other services but has its own operating and legal staff. The Bank and IDA have the same staff.

By the end of 1969, the Bank had 110 member countries, IFC 91 and IDA 102. Of the Bank's original members, Poland withdrew in 1950; Czechoslovakia failed to pay its full subscription and was expelled in 1954; Cuba and the Dominican Republic withdrew in 1960. The Dominican Republic rejoined in 1961. Indonesia, which first joined the Bank in 1954, withdrew in 1965 and was readmitted in 1967.

The total loans made by the World Bank to mid-1969 were $12,622 million. Asia and the Middle East have accounted for the largest slice, $4,215 million, and electric power has absorbed more borrowings than any other sector.

IDA's total credits have amounted to $2,170 million with Asia and the Middle East taking well over half.

173

Chapter 18

HOW THE NEW 'WORLD MONEY' WORKS

The new 'world money' or 'paper gold', technically known as Special Drawing Rights, was introduced on January 1, 1970. Until then all borrowings from the International Monetary Fund had had to be repaid. The IMF could not create money, though it did increase the total of international money (or liquidity) by swapping funds between countries. The *new* drawing rights differed from the ordinary drawing rights of the IMF in that only part of them had to be repaid. The rest in effect is a newly created asset. Thus, in issuing SDRS, the Fund stepped beyond its original concept and started to *create* new money. A unit of SDRS is equivalent to one US dollar and is defined in terms of gold.

The first distribution of SDRS, agreed by the IMF at its twenty-fourth annual meeting in September, 1969, amounted to a total of $9,500 million. Of this $3,500 million is being distributed in 1970, the rest being spread over 1971 and 1972. ($3,000 million in each year.) The UK allocation is $410 million. The total of $9,500 million compares with total world reserves (including gold, foreign exchange and IMF resources) of around $75,000 million.

These SDRS can be used in three ways. In the first place they can immediately be added to a country's gold and exchange reserves. Secondly, central banks (like the Bank of England, for example) can use them to settle debts directly between themselves. Thirdly, central banks can use them through the IMF, with the Fund designating a participant country (with a strong payments position) to receive them in exchange for its currency. Whichever method is used, the SDRS are ultimately subject to a 70 per cent rule. This lays down that countries are only allowed to keep an average of 70 per cent of the drawing rights that they have been credited with over the three-year period. Britain,

174

for example, has received some $410 million of SDRs and her reserves can be written up by that amount. (That is their value can be increased by that amount.) Provided that the average amount of the $410 million actually used does not exceed $287 million, no repayment will be necessary. But if towards the end of the period, it appears that the total used is going to be above $287 million, she will have to buy back her SDRs from other countries (using her other reserves to do so) in order to reduce her average. Thus out of the original $410 million, $287 million is a permanent addition to her own reserves, while the rest is a very temporary loan that has to be repaid.

There is one further point to notice. Until now we have been talking in terms of dollars. Actually SDRs are not necesarily drawn in any one currency. A country wanting to use SDRs would have to convert them into a currency. It might want dollars, or it might equally want marks or francs. If Britain decided that it wanted, say, $200 million worth of its permitted total, half in marks and the other half in francs, the IMF would ask the two central banks of France and Germany to credit the Bank of England with the required amount of currency and debit Britain with $200 million of her SDRs. These SDRs would then be credited to France and Germany, Britain would be charged a moderate rate of interest on the SDRs it had used and Germany and France would be paid interest at that rate.

Chapter 19

HOW THE CITY WORKS

The 'City of London', otherwise known as the 'Square Mile', is more than a location on the map. It has become a shorthand term for the financial and commercial centre of London: the equivalent of 'Wall Street' in New York. It is made up of banks, insurance companies, (including Lloyd's), shipping brokers, commodity dealers, investment trusts, export houses, Stock Exchange dealers, and financial experts of all kinds.

It is the hub of Britain's domestic financial affairs. It is also one of the leading financial centres of the world. For several kinds of business (insurance, shipping brokerage, commodity dealings) it claims more *international* transactions than any other centre. It has more foreign banks than New York or Paris and London banks have more overseas branches than banks in other centres. Thus, in spite of a succession of sterling crises since the war, the City of London has continued to expand its international business, and hence its earnings. At the last official count, its earnings in foreign exchange (i.e. its contribution to Britain's balance of payments) had almost reached £350 million. This was for 1968 and compared with just over £250 million for 1967, a little over £200 million for 1965 and £150 million for 1956. One unofficial estimate has put the 1946 total at around £50 million.

The way in which this 'invisible income' was earned can be seen from the following table:

	1965	1968
	(£ millions)	
Insurance	80	177
Banking	32	40
Merchanting	30–35	30–35
Investment Trusts, etc.	25	48
Brokerages, etc.	28	42
	205–210	337–342

It is the variety of services offered in such a small area that gives the 'Square Mile' its chief characteristics. It is not actually a square, rather a strange oblong, but it covers little more than a square mile and, as a result, contains banks, insurance offices, commodity dealers and shipping brokers all within walking distance of each other. This is its convenience. Money can be left there overnight and still earn a rate of interest (a rare offering in other financial centres). And once the money needs to be used to finance trade, or for some other commercial transaction, the other services are available virtually across the street.

This convenience has been built up over the centuries, but it finally came to fruition in the nineteenth century, at a time when the Napoleonic wars had temporarily undermined rival financial centres in Europe, when Britain's industrial machine was supplying exports to the world and earning surplus funds as an important by-product, when the Empire countries India, Australia, South Africa, Malaya, were in need of banking services and when London had become the centre not only of an Empire, but of a financial network that spanned the globe.

It is this international flavour that still dominates the London scene. As we have already seen, the world's leading gold market is established there. Lloyd's of London and the insurance companies still do more *international* business than their foreign rivals. The Baltic Exchange claims to do between a half and two-thirds of the world's merchant shipping 'fixtures' (i.e. the marrying of ships available for cargoes with potential customers). The Stock Exchange maintains daily links with leading financial centres. The banks, particularly the British overseas banks, have over 5,000 branches in all parts of the world (New York banks, though with larger overseas investments, have little more than 300). The commodity markets still provide world prices for many leading commodities. And the centre of the Eurodollar market (the most recently established financial market, as we shall see in the next chapter) is still firmly rooted in London. In short, the City of London can at least be regarded as an important international centre offering daily competition to New York, Zurich, Amsterdam, Brussels, Paris and Frankfurt. At best, it can seriously contest the title of the world's leading monetary centre.

M 177

Chapter 20

HOW THE EURODOLLAR MARKET WORKS

A eurodollar looks no different from any other dollar; for that matter eurosterling, a euromark or eurolira are all the familiar currencies we know. The 'euro' label merely means that the currency is expatriate; that the dollars, pounds, marks and lira are deposited *outside* their country of origin. The eurodollar or, more accurately, the euro-currency market is thus an international pool of liquid capital denominated in convertible currencies. The currencies need not necessarily be deposited in Europe. Any bank, be it Canadian or Japanese, can and does take deposits in non-native currencies. As soon as they do, these deposits become part of the euro-currency pool. The market has become known as the eurodollar market simply because there are many more dollars deposited outside the United States than any other currency and because Europe has attracted a large share of them. It is estimated that about 80 per cent of all euro-funds are denominated in dollars.

There are good reasons for this. The dollar is the money symbol of the most powerful economy in the world; an increasing share of world trade is being transacted in the dollar which is also accepted as the key currency in the world's foreign exchange markets.

The origins of the euro-market can be traced back to the strong flow of dollars towards Europe in the late 1940s and early 1950s which also marked the beginning of the protracted US balance of payments deficit. Whereas Europe was recovering its financial poise (and partly because of it), both Britain and the US were to face balance of payments problems for many years ahead. This, in turn, led to restrictions on capital movements (i.e. on the supply of fresh capital) first by Britain and later by the US authorities, which gave a considerable boost to

178

the one free international capital market that was able to meet demands for capital.

In effect banks, say, in London were able to foresee uses for spare money just at a time when such money was becoming available. The banks were thus encouraged to attract dollars held outside the US by offering attractive interest rates (i.e. higher than was possible inside the US). As soon as they received these externally held dollars, they lent them again for a variety of uses. In this way a new supply of credit was created; and, as fresh uses were discovered and fresh customers appeared the leading banks became more active in finding such spare deposits. The new market began to expand rapidly, as borrowers, lenders and the banks, who in effect brought them together, became more conscious of the possibilities.

When the euro-dollar market first began to evolve in the form we know it in the late 1950s, most of its funds were made available by central banks whose dollar holdings rose as the US balance of payments deficit began to mount. Soon, however, the role of the central banks diminished. Latterly it is estimated that less than one quarter of all eurodollar deposits emanate from central banks. Instead, a growing share is generated by overseas based companies, multinational corporations, wealthy individuals and, of course, banks all exchanging local currencies into dollars.

Short-term and Long-term Market
There are two arms to the euromarket: 1. the eurodollar money market, which consists predominantly of short-term deposits which are lent out through a system of bank credits; 2. the euro-dollar capital, or eurobond market, in which funds are raised by the issue of medium and long-term securities to the public. This market became active following the introduction of the US interest equalization tax in 1964 which made it uneconomic for foreign borrowers to tap the New York market. Until then many non-US borrowers had raised funds on the New York market.

The Euromoney Market
The market is huge and active. Latest estimates put the pool

at around $40 billion. Several hundred banks participate and about 50 of them in Europe, Canada and Japan handle the bulk of the business. The euromarket has no fixed meeting-place but London is by far the most prominent centre. This is one reason why so many American banks have latterly opened branch offices in London.

One of the attractions of the market is that its member banks can pay higher rates on deposits and yet charge lower rates on loans than US domestic institutions. Apart from internal US banking restrictions, the key reason here is that the euro-market is a wholesale money market operating on narrow profit margins.

The minimum size of a corporate loan from a single bank is usually $500,000. The average maximum is around $5 million. Bigger amounts have been negotiated by single borrowers with groups of banks.

Loans are made from overnight to five years. The bulk of the business is in loans for up to six months; those for longer periods require more preparation. The market has facilities for extending lines of credit on a stand-by basis for revolving commitments with interest rates negotiated at each renewal period.

On the deposit side, funds are accepted for varying maturities ranging from 'call' with two days' notice to any number of months up to five years. The bulk of deposits are for periods of a year or less. The interest paid fluctuates from day to day and as in the case of any deposits tends to be higher the longer period.

Since 1966 dollar certificates of deposits have been issued by a number of banks in London. These are negotiable instruments in bearer form and, because there is a secondary market where the certificates are traded, they provide a more liquid or more readily encashable form than a straight deposit. Also the denominations of these CDs, as they have become known, are as low as $10,000 compared with the far bigger amounts required for a straight eurodollar bank deposit.

Eurodollar Capital Market
As already explained, the eurodollar capital market began to

develop from 1964 onwards and has been growing apace ever since. In 1969, international loans amounting to $2,736 million were issued. This is a market entirely outside the US in which securities denominated in dollars or other convertible currencies are issued to or placed with the public. In the beginning most of the issues were in dollars; more recently in view of the German balance of payments surplus a growing number of these issues have been denominated in Deutschmarks (see Tables III and IV)

*Table III. Growth in the Eurobond Market by Type of Borrower**

	1965	1966	1967	1968	1969
	(All in US $million equivalent)				
Central Governments	212·5	95·1	254·7	224·4	239·7
Government Guaranteed and Agencies	222·0	133·6	380·1	354·6	506·3
Municipalities	60·5	35·0	62·0	116·3	287·0
International and European Agencies	142·5	101·0	155·0	25·0	40·0
Industrial and Financial Companies:					
Straight Debt	269·4	470·5	817·7	599·8	589·6
Convertibles and with Warrants	110·0	242·0	247·0	1,810·0	1,073·5
	1,016·9	1,077·2	1,916·5	3,130·1	2,736·1

*Table IV. Growth in Eurobond Market by Currency**

	1965	1966	1967	1968	1969
	(All in US $million equivalent)				
Dollars	702·5	837·2	1,716·3	2,361·5	1,622·5
Deutsch marks	250·0	146·3	148·8	662·5	1,053·6
E.U.A.		74·1	19·0	57·0	60·0
£/DM	64·4	19·6	20·2	28·8	—
French Francs			12·2	20·3	—
	1,016·9	1,077·2	1,916·5	3,130·1	2,736·1

* By courtesy of White, Weld & Co.

These medium- and long-term debt issues take the form of straight bonds or notes or may carry the right to convert into the equity of the borrowing company at a later stage. The latter issues are known as convertibles.

181

The size of issues averages from $10 million to $25 million but flotations for up to $50 million have been known. The standard denomination is $1,000; bonds are in bearer form, i.e. no names, which are favoured among continental investors, with interest coupons attached. The majority of these bonds are listed on the Luxembourg stock exchange as it requires minimum formalities and fees.

There are certain refinements to the longer-term issues. They can take the form of notes, usually in five years; convertibles (already described); and bonds with warrants attached. These detachable warrants carry the right to switch into a given amount of equity or common stock of a company at some future date.

Eurobond borrowers are a diverse lot ranging from European governments and international institutions such as municipalities, the European Investment Bank and European Coal and Steel Community to continental governments, municipalities and of course a host of international companies including British, Japanese, French, German industrial units and, not less, overseas offshoots of American corporations.

The underwriting and selling syndicates (that is the team of banks and brokers arranging the issues) have been equally multinational with around fifteen European and US financial institutions leading the selling groups. Among the most active houses in this area are bankers S. G. Warburg & Co. and N. M. Rothschild & Sons and stockbrokers Strauss, Turnbull & Co. in London; White, Weld and Kuhn Loeb in the US; Banque de Paris et des Pays Bas in France; Deutsche Bank in Germany and Banco Commerciale Italiano in Italy.

There is no doubt that the City of London's financial expertise and its concentration of international banks has played the leading role in the development of both the short- and long-term Euromarket—the only truly international capital market.

Chapter 21

HOW TO RAISE $3,000 MILLION IN 24 HOURS

As we have already explained, the world's central bankers had to arrange monetary help for sterling (and occasionally other currencies) on several occasions throughout the 1960s. One of the most dramatic (and the largest) of such operations took place at the end of 1964. This, briefly, is how it happened.

Towards the end of November, 1964, the new Labour Government came face to face with its first sterling crisis. The reasons for this we have discussed in earlier chapters. The fact is that the pressure on the pound had become so great that Britain's gold and exchange reserves were in danger of running out. Help was needed quickly. While the Chancellor of the Exchequer, Mr Callaghan, showed no outward sign of nervousness on Wednesday, November 25th (though arriving remarkably late for lunch and sticking pointedly to tomato juice[1]) the transatlantic telephones were getting hotter and their users tenser. Lord Cromer, the then Governor of the Bank of England, with the advice of Mr Al Hayes and Mr Charles Coombs, President and Vice President of the Federal Reserves Bank of New York, had decided to try to raise $3,000 million from their central banking colleagues in Europe and elsewhere. One of the key figures, Charles Coombs ('Charliecoombs'—one word—as *The New Yorker* likes to call him) has since explained how it all happened in an interview in *The Banker* (November 1966). This is how he put it:

'The chronology of the $3 billion [US] package of sterling in November 1964 is, to the best of my recollection, roughly as follows: On November 23rd, the Bank of England raised its discount rate from 5 to 7 per cent. Perversely enough, market

---

[1] By chance, he lunched with us that day.

183

reaction to such forceful use of monetary policy by the Labour Government quickly degenerated into fears that the threat to sterling must have reached a truly crisis stage. Whether these reactions might have been averted by earlier bank rate action, more particulárly on the usual Thursday date for Bank Rate announcements, may be debated for some time to come. In any event, the sterling market situation assumed increasingly grave significance on the London afternoon—and the New York morning of Tuesday, November 24th—when a virtual avalanche of selling developed. If sterling were to be rescued, it quickly became clear that a major package of international credit assistance would be required, and I so advised President Hayes shortly before ten o'clock that morning. President Hayes immediately telephoned Chairman Martin and US Treasury officials and found that their thinking was moving along the same lines.

'On the afternoon of the 24th, the Federal Open Market Committee—meeting through a telephone conference—approved the Special Manager's recommendation of an increase in the Federal Reserve/Bank of England swap line from $500 to $750 million, on condition that credit assistance on a roughly corresponding scale could be secured from other central banks. That evening, the Export–Import Bank gave assurance of a $250 million standby facility while two foreign central banks informally indicated a sympathetic attitude. Beginning early on the morning of November 25th, President Hayes and I joined forces with Lord Cromer in explaining by telephone to the governors of other major central banks the magnitude of the danger and the urgency of immediate defensive action in the form of a massive credit package. After roughly ten hours of almost continuous telephone communication, it was announced at 2 p.m., New York time, that $3 billion [US] credit package provided by 11 countries and the BIS was at the disposal of the Bank of England. Interest in the mechanics of how the money was raised through such teamwork has unfortunately tended to obscure the more fundamental point that each central bank's decision to lend was squarely based on the character and integrity of the Bank of England and its Governor.'

184

In other words, in a crisis the world's central bankers behave like many other people, reach for the telephone and ring their friends. But the stakes are rather larger.

Chapter 22

HOW TO READ THE PRESS

As we tried to stress at the outset, this book is intended to help those anxious to follow financial and economic affairs to find their way through the jungle of jargon and technical language which has become daily more complex. The financial columns of the press are clearly the most regular channel of communication for keeping abreast on a day-to-day basis of what is going on in the international financial field. Newspapermen invariably work against the clock and also face the problem of limited space. It is therefore scarcely surprising that they have to use financial jargon, a kind of technical shorthand, to keep their readers informed on what, as we have seen, can be quite complex issues.

For this reason we felt it might be useful to give some actual illustrations of how some of the leading newspapers have treated certain major financial issues of recent times—as they happened. Should the reader come across particular puzzling phrases or jargon we trust that the index will lead him to the appropriate explanation in earlier chapters. In any case we hope that by the time the reader has reached this part of the book the ground covered in earlier chapters will have made for a better understanding of these and similar columns in the future.

We are, of course, most grateful to the individual newspapers and writers who have given their permission for these extracts to be reproduced here.

The devaluation of Mr Callaghan

BY PATRICK HUTBER

So it has come at last. The final humiliating sterling crisis for which, sick in the stomach, I and not only I had been waiting, raged for a week and has now culminated in a 14·3 per cent devaluation combined with a severe deflationary package.

* * *

What is to be said about the situation? The use of recriminations about the past, as Churchill once said, is as a guide to action in the future. Let us start by pointing out just how badly events have been handled in the past week.

Granted that the Government was in a difficult position, that it was fighting a political as well as a financial battle, and that the French were using spoiling tactics, it seems incredibly maladroit to leave all the running to the enemies of the pound.

The Prime Minister's omission of the ritual assurances about devaluation at the Lord Mayor's banquet on Monday, Mr Callaghan's silence in the Commons on Thursday, when these are contrasted with the flood of inspired reports from the Continent, of course, a run develops and a problem turns into a crisis.

Mr Callaghan is said to be surprised that his Thursday performance had the result it did. I can't think why he should be: I or any of my colleagues or anyone in a responsible position in the City could have told him its inevitable results. I see in this, as in so many other things the Government has done, a maladroitness of touch which is fatal to the best of intentions.

Second, all those who said: 'Don't believe the Treasury forecasts' have

been proved right once again. Mr Callaghan has given the appearance of being a strong Chancellor. Strong in personality he certainly is, strong in his influence on his colleagues. But above all strong in absorbing like a sponge a Treasury viewpoint, making it his own and presenting it with immense force and vigour.

Already, incidentally, I notice a sharp change in the tone of unofficial comment. Those of us who have believed a devaluation to be necessary have never considered more than a 10 to 15 per cent drop in the exchange rate to be necessary.

This is the suggested change which has been so vehemently denounced on so many occasions. Suddenly this becomes a 'moderate' devaluation, so that, now that it has been adopted instead of something much larger, it has become, like the housemaid's baby, only a little one and thus hardly worth talking about—almost in fact a victory for the *status quo*.

It must be said, incidentally, that there could be no possible justification for a 30 per cent devaluation, which unlike a smaller one, would have shattered the world's monetary relationships and risked causing grave harm. Recklessness and pique would have been the only possible explanation of such a move.

But none of these points, significant though they are, compare in importance with the main issue that for the past three years the Government has chosen to crucify itself—and us—on the cross of a fixed exchange rate.

It has had three opportunities before this weekend to devalue in circum-

187

stances far more favourable than obtained yesterday.

The first was when it first came to office in 1964. I do not altogether blame it for rejecting the chance then. Its majority was precarious, and although it played up—disastrously—the '£800 millions deficit' it inherited from the Tories it may well have felt that the crisis was largely a temporary one of confidence.

The second opportunity was in July 1966 when it chose instead an orthodox deflationary 'package' of the most conservative (with a small c) variety.

The third, and far the most favourable, opportunity was in April this year, after three months in which gold had been flowing into the reserves. It would then have been a wholly voluntary step, taken from a position of relative strength.

At that stage the deflation was complete. No additional moves would have been required and devaluation could have provided a 'virtuous' export-led reflation. Instead we had the old familiar reflationary measures such as HP relaxation at home.

How Ministers must wish—at least how I hope they wish—they had taken the opportunity then. The whole posture of this country would have been completely different today. The Common Market negotiations would have been entered into again from a position of strength instead of weakness: as it is, General de Gaulle has been able to show, merely by lifting his little finger, just how desperate our financial position was as long as we remained pegged to the $2.80 exchange rate. How humiliating! How ludicrous!

The Government's final mistake has been more fundamental even than any of these, because it has extended over the past three years. It has desperately sought to improve the efficiency of industry—heaven knows this was desperately required—and has introduced many measures which will, over a period of time, have their effect—along with others such as the changes in the taxation system, which are a good deal less helpful.

But the essence of all these measures, such as promoting mergers, encouraging industrial training, is that they take time to have an effect. Many of them will not really bear fruit before the seventies.

But all along the Government seems to have been expecting them to have an instant, miraculous effect. There seems to have been almost a primitive belief in magic, like the idea that once unemployment was in the 2 to $2\frac{1}{2}$ per cent range, instead of the $1 \cdot 8$ per cent that has been the post-war average, wage inflation would automatically stop, and all would automatically be well.

Well, it has not proved to be so. Apart from the devaluation of the pound we are also witnessing the devaluation of Mr Callaghan.

And because he identified himself so closely with these policies that is no bad thing.

Let me end on a more cheerful note, I personally believe that a devaluation has been the missing ingredient in the Government's mix, that everything else that was done may have been necessary, but was not sufficient.

Devaluation brings the opportunity of relief from the balance of payments strait-jacket in which this country has struggled for at least the past three years. It is not an easy option but it offers the opportunity of having a genuinely growth-based economy, with industry operating to its full potential.

We may yet live to bless the day the Government's hand was forced.

From The *Sunday Telegraph*, November 18, 1967

Business

MONEY
It Could Be Dawn

Sitting with the Western world's chief central bankers as they weighed the gold crisis last week in Washington was a saturnine Frenchman who still bears the scars of his days as a Buchenwald prisoner. Though Pierre-Paul Schweitzer, 55, spoke rarely, he got undivided attention when he did. As managing director of the 107-nation International Monetary Fund—which acts as an arbiter of exchange rates, guardian of fiscal good behaviour among sovereign states, and rescue squad for countries in financial trouble—Schweitzer holds a pivotal role not only in the present struggle to shore up the world's money system but also in the reforms that seem certain to come.

With Schweitzer's full approval, the central bankers of the US and six other leading industrial nations revised a key part of the world's monetary rules. They agreed to stop buying and selling gold, and to use their remaining store of the precious metal only to settle debts between nations. Thus out of their hastily called weekend meeting was born a two-tier pricing system for gold. For central-bank exchanges of gold and dollars, the familiar $35-per-oz. price continues. For speculators, hoarders and industrial users, the price was freed to find its own level in the world's market places.

It was a case of the rescue squad arriving barely in time. The international monetary system was like a man who falls off a cliff and lands on a tree on the way down—bruised and shaken, but alive and susceptible to recovery. More auspiciously, the bankers' decision gave new urgency to the hitherto torpid efforts to turn the creaking system of international exchange into something better fit for today's world.

Fear & Faith. The international monetary system—the agreed way of exchanging one currency for another—runs on faith. For 24 years, the bulwark of that system has been the US Treasury's pledge to redeem dollars held by foreign governments for gold, at an unchanging $35 per oz. Other countries value their own money in terms of dollars, usually keep a big part of their reserves in dollars. After World War II, as other nations gradually followed the US into currency convertibility and trade liberalization, those relationships helped build an enormous, dollar-based world market. Foreigners were delighted to have the mighty dollar—until fear began to erode faith in its strength.

The source of doubt lies in statistics that concern the average American little, but worry bankers, oil sheiks, speculators and most foreign governments profoundly. In 17 of the past 18 years, the US has spent, lent or given away more money than it has taken in from abroad. Compared with the size of the US economy (larger than all of Europe's), that balance of payments deficit seems trivial; it has averaged a mere 0·004% of the gross national product. But the dollars thus placed in foreign hands now total $34 billion, while the US stock of gold has dwindled from a postwar peak of $24·6 billion to $10·4 billion last week, the thinnest gold line since 1936. If all the dollar holders demanded gold at once, there would be too little in Fort Knox to satisfy even a third of them. Already whetted, the speculative appetite for gold was only sharpened by the fall of the British pound last November.

The result was the greatest gold rush

189

in history. Almost all of the demand fell upon the London gold pool, through which the central banks of the US, Britain, West Germany, Switzerland, Italy, Belgium and The Netherlands had for 6½ years maintained the free-market price of bullion at its $35-per-oz. monetary level. Between Britain's November 18th devaluation and March 15th, when the London market was closed at the US's request, the buying stampede drained the pool of some $2·5 billion of gold—nearly 2½ times the amount mined in California during the 25 years from the gold rush to 1874. That amounted to almost 9% of the gold reserves of the seven countries; the US, having provided 59% of the pool's gold since France dropped out last summer, lost $1·5 billion. An estimated $2 billion went into the hands of speculators who were betting that the US would raise the price of gold and so hand them a swift profit.

By their decision to leave the official price intact while abandoning the gold pool, the seven nations pulled a 24-karat rug out from under the hoarders. As Zurich Banker Hans J. Baer put it: 'The central banks are saying to the speculators: "Take it to the dentist."' With the London gold market, the world's largest, closed until April 1st, the demand for gold dropped abruptly last week in smaller markets elsewhere. In Zurich, gold bars that brought $43 per oz. at the start of the week sold for $39.25 by week's end. In Paris, where the price had shot up to a record $44.36 the week before, the cost of fine gold declined to $37.89 at midweek before rebounding to $38.95.

Temptation to Profit. Welcome as the stabilizing influence of the two-price market was on both sides of the Atlantic, most bankers and economists considered it only a temporary solution to the world's monetary malaise. 'All we've bought is a bit more time,' said President John E. Whitmore of Houston's Texas National Bank of Commerce. Others were considerably more optimistic. West Germany's Economics Minister Karl Schiller maintained that the split-price arrangement 'can endure a very long time'.

The decisive element is how long the gap between gold's monetary price and its free-market price remains small. For the present, the latest $2 billion of gold to reach private hands creates a price-depressing oversupply in the market. If the free price rises to $45 per oz. or more, as some European moneymen predict, it may tempt some nations to sell official gold for the profit. Hoping to prevent that, the US last week made it clear that its gold window will be shut to governments that refuse to co-operate with the new system. Could a central bank dump gold on the free market secretly? 'Impossible,' insisted German Bundesbank President Karl Blessing. 'It would become known in twelve hours at the latest.'

Though they sprang it on speculators as a surprise, central bankers had been quietly discussing the shutdown of the London gold pool and the move to the split-price system since British devaluation. Italy and Belgium, restive at the growing drain on their reserves, remained in the pool only at US prodding. Timing the switch presented delicate problems. By waiting for repeal of a 1945 law requiring a 25% gold backing for the currency, the US could muster another $10·4 billion of gold for the defense of the dollar abroad. By discomfitingly small margins, the measure squeaked through Congress just in time. Last week, as the scratch of President Johnson's pen abolished the gold cover, the depleted US gold stock just equaled the required 25%.

From *Time*, March 29, 1968

AS LONDON REOPENS . . .

CITY
BY PATRICK SERGEANT

What price Gold?

At 10.30 this morning, in the gold-fixing room at Rothschild's, under one of the City's most charming chandeliers, the London Gold Market will begin a new phase of its life.

The men who represent the five bullion houses will be fighting to re-establish London as the world's leading centre.

They will not have been helped by the silly official decision to close the London market for the fortnight between the Gold Pool ending in Washington and last week's Stockholm conference.

President Johnson's key speech last night (to us it was the lazy, leaden-stepping hours of early morning) will affect today's gold price more than the isolation of France at Stockholm.

London dealers expect much talk but little business today. They think gold will stay at around $38 an ounce, which is an awful disappointment to people who bought hundreds of millions of pounds-worth at $35 and paid dearly for their borrowed money.

A market involves two-way traffic. Supplies are needed as well as a regular demand. London's supplies will come from Commonwealth producers and, to begin with, the people who bought vast quantities just before the Gold Pool ended a fortnight ago cannot pay for it and must sell.

The market's indigestion is huge. South Africa supplies about three-quarters of the gold mined each year in the non-Communist world.

In its last four days (March 11–14) the Gold Pool supplied buyers with the equivalent of a year's South African sales.

In less than the four months between devaluation and its end the pool supplied as much as South Africa sells in four years.

However, indigestion passes. It is not easy to kill a cat by choking it with cream.

What I found surprising was the way the gold price managed to rally in the week after the Gold Pool closed. However, the sellers are still there and I would not expect much excitement in gold, or in gold shares, until the speculators have been shaken out, which will take some time.

By then we shall have seen President Johnson's peace initiative and its success.

Deficit

In Stockholm, the Americans were saying that the initiative must come sooner than later if the President is to win the nomination let alone the election.

The US team also stirred interest with their very firm assurances about reducing their vast deficit while not retiring into an isolation that would be a disaster for the rest of us. This was also read as a portent of a sincere and successful peace initiative which, incidentally, was behind Wall Street's strength on Friday.

The Stockholm agreement on Special Drawing Rights or paper gold is an important step on the way to useful, though still distant, reform.

It will not produce at once any real resources for Germany and other

191

countries in surplus to finance the huge US payments deficit which now looks out of control.

US financial leaders worsened their state by doggedly repeating our mistakes. In trying to shock their folks at home into an austerity programme, they also terrified foreign holders of dollars. These, naturally, believe a Finance Minister who not only admits, but proclaims, that his economy is in a terrible mess.

Trade

France's determination to use the weakness of the dollar in her fight with America has finally pushed her Common Market partners to side with the US. They want to keep the Americans in Europe and are frightened of what US isolationism would do to world trade.

But in upsetting everyone the French Finance Minister asked some serious and important questions about the international system, on which I reported last week. Isolating France does not answer them. Paper gold won't. Someone should—all I learnt from economic history is that the minority is always right.

From The *Daily Mail*, April 1, 1968

THE MONEY CRISIS—
it happened because everyone broke the rules

**SPOTLIGHT by City Editor Robert Head
on the problems that face the finance chiefs**

Buss und Bet-tag—the day to Repent and Pray—is the name of the Protestant public holiday which conveniently closed Germany's banks and money markets yesterday at the height of the great currency crisis.

Desperate Finance Ministers of the main Continental nations, including Britain, seized the excuse to shut down most of their own money markets while they wrestled with the chaos at their meeting in Bonn.

From Peking, a Communist Chinese official news agency gloated: 'The monetary system of the capitalist world is sick to the core and one the verge of collapse.'

All must pray that this is no more than a wishful thought on the part of Chairman Mao.

* * *

Just after the 1939–45 war, the free nations of the world decided that they would all pull together to make sure that the chaos of the slump-ridden 1930s could never happen again.

They built a complex international machinery designed to set every democratic nation free to follow whatever policies its voters chose, without constantly looking over their shoulders at what more powerful neighbours might think.

Gold, the ancient form of money, was to be pushed into the back seat.

Elaborate

Bitter past experience had shown that when democratic governments did things that rich and powerful citizens disliked, those citizens had a nasty habit of wrecking their government's plans by changing their paper money into gold and sometimes getting it out of the country.

To free themselves from the 'tyranny' of gold, nations set up an elaborate system of fixed exchange rates so that £1 could always be swapped for an exact number of dollars, Deutschemarks, francs and so on.

This would lead to an atmosphere of certainty on which steadily growing world trade could be based.

* * *

The system might have worked beautifully for ever—if only every government could have been trusted to obey the rules.

BRITISH governments broke them regularly for nearly twenty years by overspending at home on a clumsy form of Welfare State and abroad on propping up a long dead empire east of Suez.

This led to last year's devaluation of the pound.

AMERICA broke the rules by massive spending on foreign aid, the Space race, and Vietnam.

FRANCE broke the rules when de Gaulle's overweening pride made him ignore the growing demand of his own people for a better life while his ministers sniped continually at the hated dollar and pound.

N

GERMANY broke the rules by taking the opposite attitude to most of the others and being too successful.

The ultra-conservative Germans, hag-ridden by nightmare memories of the runaway inflation which helped bring Hitler to power, have been prepared to sacrifice almost anything to uphold the value of the mark.

Strong
The strong economy this produced resulted in vast export surpluses and sucked into Germany's coffer enormous reserves at the expense of their neighbours.

Every government has tried tinkering with its economy to straighten things out at home. But they all come up against the fact that ordinary people no longer behave as they are supposed to.

For example, Chancellor Roy Jenkins's tough March budget failed to end the spending spree because many people raided their savings to meet their extra bills and taxes.

Conversely, when Germany tried to pump more spending money into their economy last year the frugal Germans merely added to their savings nesteggs.

For a time, the pressures on currencies can be smoothed over by government assurances. But, in the end, they pile so high that governments and their state banks are overwhelmed.

Everyone blames the speculators for selling weak currencies and buying strong ones in a sordid and unpatriotic attempt to make quick profits.

But far more powerful than the speculators are the huge pressures built up by ordinary people going about their daily business.

In most firms engaged in overseas trade these are clerks and executives whose job it is to buy dollars, francs, marks or sterling to pay for imported raw materials and machinery or to settle overseas bills.

If they do not protect their company from loss by buying, say, marks early and delaying their purchases of suspect currencies like francs or pounds as long as possible, then they are not doing their jobs and might face the sack.

Chaos
In the end, the present chaos will have to be resolved by drastic and permanent measures on an international level.

The money men now meeting in Bonn must agree that one day there will be a permanent realignment of exchange rates with probably the Deutschemark being upvalued against the dollar and the franc and possibly the pound devalued.

Or they will have to devise some completely new system, based perhaps on exchange rates that fluctuate day by day.

The time for papering over the cracks is running out.

From The *Daily Mirror*, November 21, 1968

Bankers in fight to stop fresh money crisis

Financial Correspondent

BASLE, Sunday

Currency markets may close again this week if the Central Bank Governors fail to reassure banks and investors in Europe that their money is safe and could not be better invested elsewhere.

At the worst, another Bonn-style conference may have to be convened and kept in session until a better and more permanent solution to Europe's financial problems can be arranged.

Central Bankers almost always delay a statement until their formal meeting on Monday, after they have consulted their Governments.

They gave no hint of agreement tonight after another long day of discussions. Sir Leslie O'Brien, Governor of the Bank of England, in the past a source of some oblique reassurance, would say nothing.

Leaving his hotel for dinner, he ran across tramlines to avoid making a comment.

With business due to begin well before the formal meeting of the Bank for International Settlements in Basle just before noon tomorrow, the foreign exchange markets look set for a nervous start.

Threat to £

If speculators read the silence as a failure to agree the pound will come under pressure.

Holders of sterling and, to a lesser extent, holders of French francs and of dollars, will need positive action of some kind tomorrow.

The confidence which was partially restored after the Basle and Bonn conferences last month was short-lived.

The outflow of 'hot' money from Germany slowed, and on Wednesday stopped. On Thursday and Friday the Bank of England was buying sterling with dollars from its reserves.

Oil sheikhs and Swiss bankers and others were selling out of pounds and dollars and buying back into marks.

The situation was made worse by the political rumours which circulated in London on Friday. One bank source here described the effect of these rumours on sterling as 'ruinous'.

But the rumours cannot entirely explain the return of a crisis atmosphere only two weeks after the Bonn conference, which showed the Governments of France and West Germany were unwilling to change the relative values of their currencies.

Return to funds

The best hope for the formal meeting in Basle tomorrow would be a promise of a scheme to identify movements of speculative money from one currency to another and offset them by returning the funds between the Central Banks of the countries concerned.

Such a scheme could work through a central organization, such as the Bank of International Settlements.

Unfortunately, it is likely to lead, under present conditions, to a steady payment of funds from the German and Swiss Central Banks to those of France and Britain.

195

This involves a degree of commitment which only governments can give and accept.

Buying time

If such a solution cannot be agreed, a fresh loan or credit for Britain, increasing the Bank of England's borrowing rights in foreign currency, might buy more time for a more permanent solution.

A further credit for sterling, whether it is absolutely essential or not, should not be ruled out. It is almost the least that will help the situation.

From The *Daily Telegraph*, December 9, 1968

The rush into D-marks goes on

BY IAN DAVIDSON

A massive flow of funds into West Germany yesterday exerted fresh pressure on sterling, the French franc and other European currencies, amid mounting speculation on a revaluation of the D-Mark.

According to estimates in the foreign exchange market in Frankfurt, about $300m. may have poured into Germany during the day, largely through the Euro-dollar market. This would bring the total inflow since the beginning of the month to an estimated $1,000m.

In London the foreign exchange market was described as chaotic. Spot sterling closed unchanged on balance close to the floor at $2·38$\frac{5}{16}$, and it is understood that slightly more support by the Bank of England may have been required than on Tuesday.

The forward market was considerably weaker, however. In London, the three-month discount at one point reached the abnormally high level of 8$\frac{1}{2}$ cents, and closed at 6$\frac{1}{2}$ cents, which was 2$\frac{3}{32}$ cents up on the day. In New York the three months discount was quoted at 8$\frac{1}{2}$ cents at the close.

Day-to-day sterling was costing the equivalent of an effective rate of 100 per cent per annum, while the annual rate for week-end borrowing approached 70 per cent. It is understood that some banks may have refused to give forward cover for some of their commercial clients because of the disorderly state of the market.

The speculation on a possible D-Mark revaluation was given further impetus by a speech by the German Government spokesman, Dr Conrad Ahlers. He told a meeting of businessmen in Stuttgart on Tuesday night that the decision on whether to revalue the D-Mark should be taken soon, 'and it could fall either for or against revaluation'.

* * *

All eyes are now fixed on next week-end's meeting of central bankers at the Bank for International Settlements in Basle, when the international currency situation is bound to be discussed. Earlier this year they agreed on the outlines of a plan for recycling hot-money flows so as to counter speculative movements, and while there appear to be some differences of opinion between the creditors and debtors over the automaticity of the plan, they will be under considerable pressure to take effective action this week-end.

German reluctance to revalue is based largely on the Government's view that a parity change would be an unpopular move in an election year, but Dr Ahlers' remarks yesterday suggest that the speculative build-up and the continuing state of tension are producing some strains in the coalition Cabinet.

* * *

It may be significant, moreover, that Dr Ahlers omitted the demand which has been included in all previous Ministerial statements that the D-Mark could only be revalued as part of a multilateral realignment, with the clear implication that the French franc would be devalued.

At this stage it still seems unlikely that the French franc will be devalued before the coming presidential elections. If M. Georges Pompidou were confident of being elected—and he is a strong favourite at the moment—he

197

might be ready to acquiesce in a devaluation which took place before polling day, June 1st. But the present caretaker Government of M. Maurice Couve de Murville is unlikely to agree to such a step without a firm promise that it would continue in office under the next President. Moreover, it is still possible that the interim President, M. Alain Poher, may decide to stand as a Centrist candidate, and thus upset all pre-ballot predictions.

The West German Economics Minister, Herr Schiller is going to Washington on May 16th and 17th, it was announced in Bonn yesterday. The visit has been planned for several weeks and has no direct connection with present uncertainty.

NEW YORK VIEWS

By Samuel Brittan, Economics Editor
NEW YORK, May 7th

Foreign exchange market fears of a major currency crisis have dominated trading here today. Everyone has been rushing to buy Deutschemarks, and the mark and sterling have been the only currencies in which it has been possible to trade to an appreciable extent—a very remarkable situation.

The strongly held view in the New York financial community is that a decision on the German mark and French franc parities cannot be postponed much longer. The regular meeting at Basle this week-end is bound to attract enormous attention, and it will be extremely difficult to find any form of words after the meeting that will calm the market.

Two schools
There are two schools of thought on

the implications for sterling. Many bankers and Stock Exchange men are dubious about the situation of the pound. The table in the Financial Statement published on Budget Day, showing short- and medium-term debts of £3,600m., together with more recent figures showing that the UK is still running a current deficit, are to be found on bankers' desks.

On the other hand, basic British policies still meet with warm approval in central banking circles in New York, which are at a loss to understand the disappointing results so far. The New York Federal Reserve was known to be fiercely opposed to the November, 1967, devaluation and is inclined to draw the moral that exchange rate changes should be avoided. On the other hand, the attitude both to the problems of sterling and to flexible exchange rates generally is a shade less rigid than was common even a little while ago.

$ linchpin
Among private bankers a strong movement is growing up in favour of some exchange rate flexibility; but it is thought that the dollar, as the linchpin of the system, cannot be the currency to float.

In the market the first three days of the week have been noticeable much more for a run into Deutschemarks—from a variety of currencies including the dollar—than for a rush out of sterling.

The Bank of England has apparently taken most of the pressure on the rate rather than on the reserves. The French franc for its part seems to have been protected to some extent by the stringent exchange controls.

From *The Financial Times*, May 8, 1969

FRANCE FREEZES NEARLY ALL PRICES AS INFLATION CURB

Acts to Prevent Widespread Increases Expected in Wake of Devaluation

BAN STAYS TO SEPT. 15

14 Nations in Africa Follow Paris's Lead in Reducing Worth of Currencies

BY JOHN L. HESS

Special to *The New York Times*

PARIS, Aug. 10—The French Government today ordered a freeze on prices to accompany the devaluation of the franc, which became formal at 10 o'clock tonight (5 p.m. New York time).

It decreed that virtually all industrial prices and nearly all markups by wholesalers and retailers be blocked at the levels of last Friday, before the surprise announcement of devaluation. The freeze was made effective until September 15th.

The devaluation was matched tonight by the 14 African countries of the franc zone. Their decision, announced after a meeting of their representatives with Finance Minister Valéry Giscard d'Estaing, had been regarded as inevitable.

Left-Wing Complaints

Widespread price increases had been expected today in a classic reaction of businessmen to the prospect that the cost of imports was automatically going up 12·5 per cent, and that nearly all other costs would be affected sooner or later. Jewelers in resort towns were reported to have raised prices yesterday.

An abrupt increase in living costs would have confirmed complaints of labor unions and left-wing elements generally—including some Gaullists—that the problem of the franc was being settled at the expense of the poor, while the wealthy would make windfall profits.

By September 15th the Government plans to have a package of economic and relief measures ready for administrative action and for a special session of Parliament.

Wage Increase Expected

The franc was devalued to 18·004 United States cents from 20·225 cents. The devaluation is 12·5 per cent for the Frenchman who wants to buy foreign currency, but amounts to 11·1 per cent in terms of gold or the dollar.

Premier Jacques Chaban-Delmas made clear in a radio interview tonight that the Government was sensitive to the situation of people of low income.

How France Kept Devaluation Secret

BY HENRY GINIGER

Special to *The New York Times*

PARIS, Aug. 10—Despite controversy over France's devaluation of the franc, there is nothing but admiration—in some cases grudging—for the way it was carried out.

The devaluation was a tight secret until the moment it was announced

199

late Friday afternoon. The extent of the surprise was indicated by the first reaction of a local banker who admitted that even his expert world had been caught off guard.

Everyone concerned knew the franc was in trouble, and the general thinking was that sooner or later devaluation could not be avoided. But none of the elements that usually accompany such an act were present: no immediate crisis, no speculative movement of great dimension and no rumors flying about to be met by official denials that are often interpreted as confirmations.

President Pompidou and his ministers saw their country's reserves continually leaving France, so decided to act in advance of a full-blown crisis, while they still had a cushion.

Finance Minister Valéry Giscard d'Estaing said that he went to see the President privately after a full Cabinet meeting July 16th, and the decision was made then.

Choosing a dull summer month when financial and business activity is at its lowest point of the year and when many Europeans are vacationing was the first element of surprise.

The second element was to limit knowledge of the decision to as few people as possible. The Finance Minister said that until last Wednesday eight persons were concerned with preparations for the devaluation.

From *The New York Times*, August 11, 1969

Bonn announces 9·29 pc revaluation after disturbed day in markets

BY IAN MORISON, Banking Correspondent

The Deutsche Mark is being revalued by just over 9¼ per cent. Karl Schiller, West Germany's Economics Minister, announced last night that the parity would move from 4 to 3·66 marks to the dollar at midnight on Sunday. As a result German imports will be 8·5 per cent cheaper and exports 9·2896 per cent more expensive. However, the concomitant removal of the 4 per cent tax will lessen the blow for German exporters.

The new rate chosen is at the higher end of the range of parities which have been considered probable since the intention to revalue first became apparent. Yesterday the world's foreign exchange markets had a disturbed day as expectations of a relatively large revaluation grew and speculative money moved into the mark and the Dutch guilder.

At the old fixed rate there were 9·6 marks to the pound, with each mark worth 2s. 1d. The new figures will be 8·78 and 2s. 3·3d. respectively.

Tight credit policy may be eased
Patricia Lloyd Jones writes from Frankfurt: The new official parity of the Deutsche Mark is seen as a compromise between the wishes of German industry and the counsel of those who fear that a too modest revaluation would be an invitation to the world to call for a further revaluation in the near future. The big question now is what kind of supporting economic measures will the new Government announce in its declaration to the Bundestag on Tuesday.

It has been rumoured that the Government will appeal to the Bundesbank to relax its tight credit policy. This would help to ease the pressure on business and the credit system in the next weeks as foreign money pours out of Germany and act as an incentive to German producers to turn their attention to the home market.

Government considers aid
In addition the Government might move to assess industrial branches which have suffered from the revaluation and give support to underdeveloped business branches and backward geographic areas. In a televised speech to the nation last night the Economics Minister, Professor Schiller, indicated that such a programme would be developed if needed.

However, the realization of Professor Schiller's aim of turning German industry inward to the domestic market by fostering steady growth and expansion depends very much on whether the Bundesbank is willing to go along by relaxing its restrictive credit policy.

Most west German industrialists were apprehensive. 'The revaluation is being regretted by the industry, but accepted', an official of the Industry Federation said. The largest exporters, including the car, consumer goods and shipbuilding industries, would be hit by higher prices for their exports.

The Automobile Industry Federation said it did not expect an immediate drop in exports. A spokesman for the Shipbuilders' Federation called for government subsidies to keep prices competitive.

Chemical industry threatened
'For the chemical industry, with an export share in total output of 37 per

cent, the mark revaluation will have serious repercussions', the Chemical Industry Federation said, and predicted sharp cuts in profits. The Machine Builders' Federation, representing the country's largest exporters, said it did not expect any immediate effects, but 'for the future we expect noticeable declines in our exports'.

The Industry Federation forecast that the DM.15,000m. trade surplus predicted for 1969 would be brought down to DM.10,000m. or DM.11,000m. in 1970. It did not expect revaluation effects to be felt this year.

The federation would not comment

officially on the move—but the spokesman said: 'We would have preferred a 6 per cent revaluation rate.'

Central Bank sources in Frankfurt said they expected that about DM.3,000m. of hot money still held by west German commercial banks would begin to flow out of the country when the foreign exchange markets opened on Monday.

Between DM.5,000m. and DM. 6,000m. had flowed out of the country since the mark was floated on September 29th as speculators who had bought marks at a cheaper rate took their profits by selling them at higher rates on the market, they said.

US welcomes the new rate
FROM PETER JAY, Economics Editor

Washington, October 24.—A statement released immediately after the news of the 9·29 per cent Deutschemark revaluation reached Washington read: 'The Treasury welcomes the announcement by the German authorities of their decision to establish a new par value for the mark at $0·2732, 9·29 per cent above their previously established par. Today's action by the German Government should resolve in a constructive manner the principal of uncertainty that has existed in the exchange markets.'

Formal approval by the board of the International Monetary Fund, which met almost immediately after the formal application was received from Bonn, was announced later.

First private reactions in official circles here were of considerable pleasure that the final decision on the amount of the revaluation had come out so near the top of the 6–10 per cent range predicted.

Judgment is still reserved whether the net effect of the revaluation, together with the removal of the border

tax adjustments of last November and the current wage explosion, will be sufficient to correct Germany's persistent current account surplus.

The United States tends to favour all revaluations because they have the effect of devaluing the dollar against the revalued currencies, thus making United States goods and services more competitive in international trade.

Philip Jacobson writes from New York: The revaluation was received calmly by New York foreign exchange markets and dealers reported that business remained light after the initial announcement. At that stage the traded dollar rate was 27·10 to 27·15 against what would be the new floor rate of 27·32. Dealers stressed that they would need full details of the west German move before they could come to any firm conclusions, but a number pointed out that, assuming the mark goes to its new floor, a heavy outflow of funds seemed inevitable.

A spokesman for Volkswagen of America Inc. told AP-Dow Jones the west German revaluation 'necessitates a review of our pricing and may mean an increase in the suggested retail list prices of our vehicles here'.

The Commerce Department said today that the United States trade surplus rose to its highest level this year in September. Seasonally adjusted it was $271m. compared with $205m. in August.

Dutch say no change in guilder

Amsterdam.—There will be no revaluation of the Dutch guilder. West Germany is Holland's biggest trade partner and in the foreign exchange markets it had been assumed that a German revaluation of over 8 per cent or so would make the guilder a strong candidate for a smaller change in parity. But last night it was announced in The Hague that there would be no revaluation.

Vienna.—Austria will not devalue the schilling, Chancellor Josef Klaus said. He made the announcement on a nation-wide radio broadcast after an afternoon meeting of the Austrian National Bank.

Brussels.—The feeling here is that revaluation of the mark will send shock waves through the European Common Market, its relations with Britain, and through the whole international monetary system.

Geneva.—Swiss bankers regard the revaluation as the maximum that was possible without one or two of the other currencies, particularly the Dutch guilder, being forced to alter parity as well.

They expect 'a strong dollar' when the markets open on Monday and that sterling also will benefit. The French franc should also be in better shape but its prospects on medium term are regarded as depending largely on the labour front situation.

Zurich.—Bankers said West Germany had revalued by the maximum amount possible without forcing other currencies to revalue.

While some immediate buying of Swiss francs is expected, Zurich bankers are convinced that speculators will soon be dissuaded.

Rome.—The revaluation of the mark caused little surprise in Italian economic circles, but there was some disagreement about whether this degree of revaluation was sufficient.

Stock market sources in Milan reported that a higher degree of revaluation had been expected.

Paris may ease credit

Paris, Oct. 24.—Valéry Giscard d'Estaing, French Finance Minister said last night that a 'softening' of the credit squeeze in France can be expected 'in the next few months'.

First reaction from a Finance Ministry official was that revaluation by 9·29 per cent is 'very satisfactory . . . it is very favourable (to France) and within the calculations made by the French Government when it decided to devalue the franc last August'.

Mercedes to raise prices

Prices of Mercedes-Benz and Auto Union Audi cars will be raised by 4 to 5 per cent, Bill Argent, managing director of Mercedes-Benz (Great Britain), said at the Motor Show in London yesterday.

He said the increase was due to the floating exchange rate for the Deutschemark and a rise in factory prices after a wage award. The revisions also would reflect the Kennedy round of tariff cuts due in January.

203

Boost to Britain's balance of payments

The revaluation of the Deutschemark should have a fairly speedy and wholly beneficial effect on the British balance of payments. In Whitehall last night, it was felt that soon there could be an improvement of between £60m. and £70m. a year, even after allowing for the removal of the 4 per cent border tax.

The impact of this revaluation will be far more pronounced than, say, that of the devaluation of the French franc because of both the greater volume of direct trade and the larger number of third markets in which Britain and German exporters compete.

The removal of a major element of currency uncertainty should be of major assistance to sterling when the foreign exchange markets open on Monday. There are still large speculative positions in marks to be liquidated and, while the Eurodollar market may prove the initial beneficiary, Britain should see its share of the money in due course.

In anticipation of the revaluation, sterling moved well ahead yesterday after falling sharply in early trading. The spot rate closed with a gain of four points at $2.3918. The mark had closed at 3.7075 to the dollar on the London market after moving below 3.7 for a time while the guilder was held at its official ceiling for most of the day only because the Dutch Central Bank reputedly absorbed some $245m. (£100m.) of foreign currency. French and Swiss francs were dull.

Industry's immediate reaction last night to the revaluation was one of relief that uncertainty surrounding the currency and its effect on international trading had been ended. The level of revaluation was much as expected.

A spokesman for the British National Export Council said last night that the extent of the revaluation was a 'pleasant surprise'. Even allowing for the abolition of the German import rebate and export tax—the effects of which had been unquantifiable anyway—the move should aid British exports against German ones.

The Board of Trade, which is expected to make a formal statement over the weekend or next week, will be urging industry to increase export effort in those areas where competition between Britain and Germany is greatest.

The London Chamber of Commerce will be mounting a series of export promotions aimed at Germany and as a first step will send a trade mission to Germany in 1970, a spokesman said last night.

Dr Bracewell Milnes, finance director of the Confederation of British Industry, said last night that the revaluation was as much as could have been hoped for. 'In general this will be beneficial to British industry', he said.

Albert Frost, finance director of Imperial Chemical Industries, said: 'We were expecting it and we made our dispositions in good time. Considering that the mark was lifted only very recently by 6 to 7 per cent and considering that the rebate on imports has gone, this revaluation will have very little effect on Germany's competitive position with this country.'

Although the revaluation is rather more than the gilt-edged market expected—the general opinion was that it would be between $6\frac{1}{2}$ and $8\frac{1}{2}$ per cent—it will probably have only a muted effect on prices of British Government securities. The removal of a currency uncertainty will naturally strengthen sentiment, and as a 9·2 per cent revaluation has probably not been fully discounted, the long and medium-dated loans are likely to be marked up $\frac{1}{4}$ or, perhaps, $\frac{1}{2}$ a point.

From *The Times Business News*, October 25, 1969

When considered alongside the changes in parity of the pound and the franc, Germany's week-end revaluation of the Mark is hardly 'chicken feed'. Yet it does not spell an end to parity changes

Revaluation: why Germany went for the top end of the scale

BY SAMUEL BRITTAN, Economics Editor

The mark revaluation must be the longest-awaited currency change there has ever been. There were two previous flights from other currencies into the mark, first in November and then in May. The first was followed by the border tax measures. Although these were nominally just over 4 per cent, they only covered visible trade in non-agricultural goods, and the net effect was that of a back-door revaluation of 3 per cent.

The third wave of speculation which hit the mark, just before the September election, was followed by a four-week period of floating, during which the mark soon moved up—with plenty of nods and winks from the Bundesbank —to the neighbourhood of the new rate. Contrary to popular belief, the period of floating did not begin on Monday, September 29th, when it was officially announced, but on the previous Thursday, September 25th, when the German foreign exchange markets were closed and the mark was allowed to find its own level in the other main centres.

Election result critical
Although the change now looks as if it was inevitable all along, the appearance is deceptive. If the Christian Democrats had gained as little as 1 per cent more of the votes—indeed, if the result had been as computer analysts were confidently claiming when we

went to bed on that Sunday night—a Christian Democrat dominated Government might still be in power, and the future of the mark still a source of bitter discord in international monetary relations.

The new mark rate is about 1 per cent higher than was indicated by the free market rate at the end of last week, and 2 per cent higher than some of the suggestions emanating from Bundesbank circles about four weeks ago. One reason why Professor Schiller moved to the high side of the probable range was a desire to have a sharper effect on the inflationary mood that has been growing up in Germany recently. German industrialists will now find it more difficult to pass on inflationary wage claims in export prices; and the opening up of the home market to cheaper imports should also put a brake on rising prices. On the financial side, the outflow of speculative funds should make it much easier to regulate the domestic money supply, and interest rates may decline slightly.

But an omelette cannot be made without breaking eggs. The inflationary boom in the year preceding the election has gathered such steam, that it will probably require some check to business activity and employment to reduce inflation. This would be true whatever anti-inflationary method were used. The advantage of revaluation is that, in contrast to domestic restriction, it

205

raises the standard of living of the German consumer.

A second reason for the relatively large revaluation is that the German authorities want to put an end for as long as possible to the whole problem of the trade surplus, the never-ending series of crises and meetings, and the constant pressure on the Federal Republic by her partners. This determination was increased when it became clear that—for the time being—a fixed-rate revaluation was all that the new German Government was prepared to contemplate. Technically there was a great deal to be said for a slightly smaller revaluation combined with the Emminger formula for a discretionary upward call.

But Germany's Common Market partners, and in particular France, together with the Brussels Commission insisted that any form of flexibility was incompatible with any hope of restoring the Common Agricultural Policy. This view was disputable on economic grounds, but the new Government was not prepared to start life with a show down with its Common Market partners on what would have seemed to many of the new Ministers a very esoteric point. Nor should one forget that Herr Blessing, the retiring head of the Bundesbank, is still at heart a fixed exchange rate man and would hardly do battle for currency novelties.

No one can know for how long revaluation will put the mark problem to rest. It is worth remembering that the 5 per cent revaluation of 1961 at first seemed to have very little effect; then it seemed if anything to have been too much, and in 1965 Germany experienced a genuine payments deficit. But a year or two later a condition of chronic surplus had once more returned.

Much more useful than any crystal gazing is to look at the full extent of the currency changes of the last couple of years. If one adds together the sterling devaluation of November 1967, and the present mark revaluation, the German currency has become some 27½ per cent more expensive, while sterling has become 24 per cent cheaper in terms of marks. Similarly, if one takes into account the French devaluation of last August the franc-mark parity has changed by 20–23 per cent. The net results can hardly be regarded as chicken feed.

Whitehall has evidently calculated that the final stage of the German revaluation which is effectively 6 per cent (8½ per cent measured one way, 9·3 per cent the other minus the abolition of the border tax measures) should eventually boost the British balance of payments by £60m.–£70m. This is worthwhile as a rough guess indicating at most the order of magnitude.

Every fixed rate currency change has a peculiar J-shaped effect on international trading balances. Because prices change very quickly, while the volume response takes much longer, the first effect of an exchange rate change is a perverse one. Surpluses, increases and deficits get worse, it takes months or years for the net effect to become favourable. The speed of the process depends on many factors, including the way in which exporters respond to currency changes, internal financial policies and the pressure on domestic capacity.

A helpful metaphor might be that of a wind tunnel along which impulses of different kinds are passed at varying speeds; and what emerges at the other end at any precise moment is an incalculable mixture. All one can say is that if the changes have been in the right direction, the eventual effect on the world balance of payments should be favourable.

From *The Financial Times*, October 27, 1969

The March issue of the US Federal Reserve Bulletin provides much the most complete account yet available of the severe currency crises which jolted the international monetary system during 1969

How much money is there in the Italian suitcase?

BY ANDREAS WHITTAM SMITH

The inside story of some of last year's great currency crises can now be told, thanks to the Federal Reserve Bank of New York, the most important element in the American central banking system. The 'Fed', as it is called, has just published a pretty full description of its own activities in 1969, which included handling the frenzied speculation on a mark revaluation and the upset caused by devaluation of the French franc.

The reason why the Fed almost always gets involved in other people's crises is that most foreign exchange dealings are done in dollars. When sterling is sold, sterling deposits are being swapped for dollar deposits. When German marks are bought dollar deposits are being sold in return for mark deposits. Both movements on a large scale are embarrassing for the central banks involved and the Fed is always one.

Thus the Federal Reserve has made arrangements with each of the major European central banks under which both sides agree to neutralize currency flows up to a certain limit. The Bank of England has the biggest limit—$2,000 millions. The central banks of Canada, France, Germany, Italy and Japan each have limits of $1,000 millions.

Altogether the facilities available under the swap system with the Federal Reserve amount to just under $11,000 millions. The swap system works both ways. It does not only consist of foreign central banks drawing on US Federal Reserve credits. At March 10, 1970, for instance, the Federal Reserve was $85 millions in debt to the Belgium national bank and $130 millions to the Netherlands.

The first big currency crisis of 1969 was the worst in terms of the size of funds involved. I refer to the unprecedented speculation on a revaluation of the mark, which started at the end of April and ended 10 days later after $4,100 millions (£1,700 millions) of foreign currencies had been pumped into Germany.

The Fed calls this 'the heaviest flow in international financial history'. It is an enormous amount. It is, for instance, considerably more than Britain's reserves of gold and foreign currency, or about the same as the market capitalization of British Petroleum, which is seventh largest in the world oil league.

* * *

What conclusions can be drawn from this detailed account of the 1969 currency crises? It shows how rapidly

207

speculative pressure can mount. The first German crisis blew up literally overnight.

This works both ways. Once a speculative situation has been pricked, currencies flow back to where they started with remarkable rapidity. The Bank of England has found this time and time again. Secondly, it reveals how large is the mass of speculative funds waiting to move from one currency to another. No government, however strong, can cope with these rushes unaided. And they are difficult to judge in advance. The Germans certainly did not intend to lose $5,000 quite so quickly as they have.

Pendulum

Thirdly, the pendulum of favour or disfavour can swing very quickly. In August Belgian francs were being sold because it was feared they would be devalued. In October the Belgian franc was being bought on hopes that it would be revalued.

Finally, it is worth noting the one currency which did badly out of every crisis—the Italian lira. The Fed puts a figure on the suitcase traffic (that is the export of Italian banknotes over the frontier into Switzerland). Net capital outflows from Italy reached $2,800 millions during 1969, of which 'fully two thirds' consisted of the export of banknotes. The Fed describes the reasons with a delicate touch, saying that 'Italian savings were attracted by the broad range of financial instruments available in foreign money and capital markets, as well as by the anonymity which foreign placements provide.'

From *The Guardian*, March 26, 1970

Index

o

Pound—*contd.*
as reserve currency, 19, 37, 38,
39, 40–3, 44, 45, 77, 139–40
as trading currency, 39
Basle Facility for, 65
devaluation, 59, 187–8
pressures on, 100–1
(*See also* sterling)
press, financial, 186–209
prices, and exports, 32
and trade balance, 32
production costs, 31
prosperity, post-war, 50
threats to, 128, 145
protectionism, 116

reserve currencies, 19, 37–8, 39, 45,
46, 77
future of, 139–40
(*See also* dollar *and* pound)
reserves, gold and foreign exchange,
15, 55
revaluation, Bretton Woods and,
133
Rhodesia, use of barter, 18
Rolfe, Sidney, 46
Roosevelt, President, 114
Rothschild, N. M. & Sons, 81, 82,
182
Rueff, Jacques, 45, 77, 161
Russia, 62
gold discoveries, 70, 156
gold payments and sales, 19, 21,
83, 86

Samuel Montagu, merchant banker,
76, 81, 83, 88
Scheduled Territories, 41, 42
Second World War, economic
recovery after, 128
Sergeant, Patrick, 192
services, payments for, 26–7
Schonfield, Andrew, 96
silver, 16, 18
Sharps, Pixley & Co., 81

Smith, Adam, 29
Smith, Andreas Whittam, 208
slump (1929) features of, 113–17
South Africa, 41
gold discoveries, 70, 80, 156
policy, 89
production, 79, 81, 83, 86
Swiss banks and, 90
South African Reserve Bank, 87
Soviet bloc, 19
Spain, 33
Special Drawing Rights (SDRs),
and international monetary
system, 61, 159–60
amount available, 159
as 'paper-gold', 61, 80, 159
first distribution, 174
initiated, 66–7, 140, 174
problems of, 140
sterling and, 66–7
use of, 174–5
speculation, against currencies,
50–1, 67
and exchange rates, 54, 55
and impending devaluations, 132
central banks and, 138
spot rate, 25
sterling, and gold standard, 39–40
and SDRs, 66–7
area, 41–3, 66, 119–23
crises, 59, 65, 130, 131, 135,
183–4
devaluation, 47, 52–3, 65, 67–8,
131, 135
dollar rate, 49, 52
emergence as world currency,
39–40
reserve currency role, 38, 40,
65–7
trading currency role, 38, 39, 40
(*See also* pound)
Stock Exchange, London, 151, 177
stock market, New York, 145–7,
151
Strauss, Turnbull, 182

215